BY FAITH

A STUDY IN THE BOOK OF GALATIANS

GLENNA MARSHALL

STUDY SUGGESTIONS

We believe that the Bible is true, trustworthy, and timeless and that it is vitally important for all believers. These study suggestions are intended to help you more effectively study Scripture as you seek to know and love God through His Word.

SUGGESTED STUDY TOOLS

- A Bible

- A double-spaced, printed copy of the Scripture passages that this study covers. You can use a website like *www.biblegateway.com* to copy the text of a passage and print out a double-spaced copy to be able to mark on easily.

- A journal to write notes or prayers

- Pens, colored pencils, and highlighters

- A dictionary to look up unfamiliar words

HOW TO USE THIS STUDY

Begin your study time in prayer. Ask God to reveal Himself to you, to help you understand what you are reading, and to transform you with His Word (Psalm 119:18).

Before you read what is written in each day of the study itself, read the assigned passages of Scripture for that day. Use your double-spaced copy to circle, underline, highlight, draw arrows, and mark in any way you would like to help you dig deeper as you work through a passage.

Read the daily written content provided for the current study day.

Answer the questions that appear at the end of each study day.

The inductive method provides tools for deeper and more intentional Bible study. To study a book of the Bible inductively, work through the steps below after reading background information on the book.

1 **OBSERVATION & COMPREHENSION**
Key question: What does the text say?

After reading the book of the Bible in its entirety at least once, begin working with smaller portions of the book. Read a passage of Scripture repetitively, and then mark the following items in the text:

- Key or repeated words and ideas
- Key themes
- Transition words (*Ex: therefore, but, because, if/then, likewise, etc.*)
- Lists
- Comparisons & Contrasts
- Commands
- Unfamiliar words (look these up in a dictionary)
- Questions you have about the text

2 **INTERPRETATION**
Key question: What does the text mean?

Once you have annotated the text, work through the following steps to help you interpret its meaning:

- Read the passage in other versions for a better understanding of the text.
- Read cross-references to help interpret Scripture with Scripture.
- Paraphrase or summarize the passage to check for understanding.
- Identify how the text reflects the metanarrative of Scripture, which is the story of creation, fall, redemption, and restoration.
- Read trustworthy commentaries if you need further insight into the meaning of the passage.

3 APPLICATION
Key Question: How should the truth of this passage change me?

Bible study is not merely an intellectual pursuit. The truths about God, ourselves, and the gospel that we discover in Scripture should produce transformation in our hearts and lives. Answer the following questions as you consider what you have learned in your study:

- What attributes of God's character are revealed in the passage?

    Consider places where the text directly states the character of God, as well as how His character is revealed through His words and actions.

- What do I learn about myself in light of who God is?

    Consider how you fall short of God's character, how the text reveals your sin nature, and what it says about your new identity in Christ.

- How should this truth change me?

    A passage of Scripture may contain direct commands telling us what to do or warnings about sins to avoid in order to help us grow in holiness. Other times our application flows out of seeing ourselves in light of God's character. As we pray and reflect on how God is calling us to change in light of His Word, we should be asking questions like, "How should I pray for God to change my heart?" and "What practical steps can I take toward cultivating habits of holiness?"

ATTRIBUTES OF GOD

ETERNAL

God has no beginning and no end. He always was, always is, and always will be.

HAB. 1:12 / REV. 1:8 / IS. 41:4

FAITHFUL

God is incapable of anything but fidelity. He is loyally devoted to His plan and purpose.

2 TIM. 2:13 / DEUT. 7:9
HEB. 10:23

GLORIOUS

God is ultimately beautiful, deserving of all praise and honor.

REV. 19:1 / PS. 104:1
EX. 40:34-35

GOOD

God is pure; there is no defilement in Him. He is unable to sin, and all He does is good.

GEN. 1:31 / PS. 34:8 / PS. 107:1

GRACIOUS

God is kind, giving to us gifts and benefits which we do not deserve.

2 KINGS 13:23 / PS. 145:8
IS. 30:18

HOLY

God is undefiled and unable to be in the presence of defilement. He is sacred and set-apart.

REV. 4:8 / LEV. 19:2 / HAB. 1:13

IMMUTABLE

God does not change. He is the same yesterday, today, and tomorrow.

1 SAM. 15:29 / ROM. 11:29
JAMES 1:17

JEALOUS

God is desirous of receiving the praise and affection He rightly deserves.

EX. 20:5 / DEUT. 4:23-24
JOSH. 24:19

JUST

God governs in perfect justice. He acts in accordance with justice. In Him there is no wrongdoing or dishonesty.

IS. 61:8 / DEUT. 32:4 / PS. 146:7-9

LOVE

God is eternally, enduringly, steadfastly loving and affectionate. He does not forsake or betray His covenant love.

JN. 3:16 / EPH. 2:4-5 / 1 JN. 4:16

MERCIFUL

God is compassionate, withholding us from the wrath that we deserve.

TITUS 3:5 / PS. 25:10
LAM. 3:22-23

OMNIPOTENT

God is all-powerful; His strength is unlimited.

MAT. 19:26 / JOB 42:1-2
JER. 32:27

OMNIPRESENT

God is everywhere; His presence is near and permeating.

PROV. 15:3 / PS. 139:7-10
JER. 23:23-24

OMNISCIENT

God is all-knowing; there is nothing unknown to Him.

PS. 147:4 / I JN. 3:20
HEB. 4:13

PATIENT

God is long-suffering and enduring. He gives ample opportunity for people to turn toward Him.

ROM. 2:4 / 2 PET. 3:9 / PS. 86:15

RIGHTEOUS

God is blameless and upright. There is no wrong found in Him.

PS. 119:137 / JER. 12:1
REV. 15:3

SOVEREIGN

God governs over all things; He is in complete control.

COL. 1:17 / PS. 24:1-2
1 CHRON. 29:11-12

TRUE

God is our measurement of what is fact. By Him are we able to discern true and false.

JN. 3:33 / ROM. 1:25 / JN. 14:6

WISE

God is infinitely knowledgeable and is judicious with His knowledge.

IS. 46:9-10 / IS. 55:9 / PROV. 3:19

CREATION

In the beginning, God created the universe. He made the world and everything in it. He created humans in His own image to be His representatives on the earth.

FALL

The first humans, Adam and Eve, disobeyed God by eating from the fruit of the Tree of Knowledge of Good and Evil. Because of sin, the world was cursed. The punishment for sin is death, and because of Adam's original sin, all humans are sinful and condemned to death.

REDEMPTION

God sent his Son to become a human and redeem His people. Jesus Christ lived a sinless life but died on the cross to pay the penalty for sin. He resurrected from the dead and ascended into heaven. All who put their faith in Jesus are saved from death and freely receive the gift of eternal life.

RESTORATION

One day, Jesus Christ will return again and restore all that sin destroyed. He will usher in a new heaven and new earth where all who trust in Him will live eternally with glorified bodies in the presence of God.

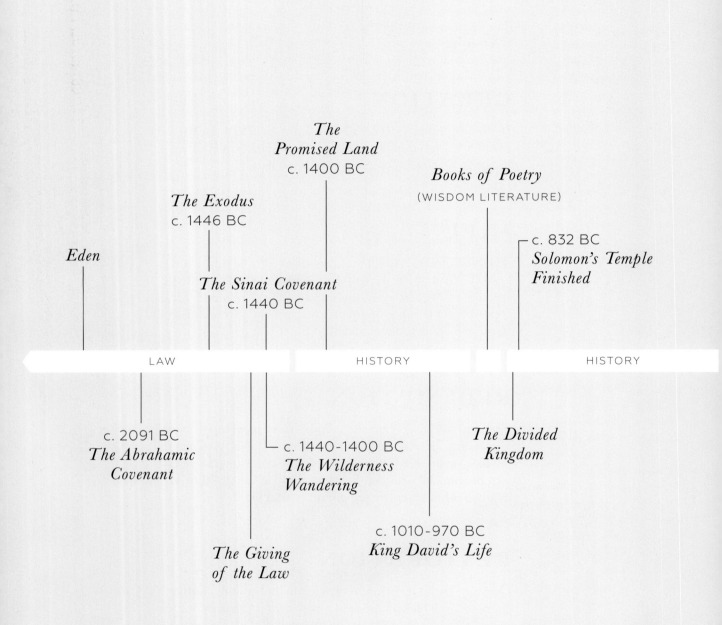

The Promised Land
c. 1400 BC

Books of Poetry
(WISDOM LITERATURE)

The Exodus
c. 1446 BC

c. 832 BC
Solomon's Temple Finished

Eden

The Sinai Covenant
c. 1440 BC

LAW   HISTORY   HISTORY

c. 2091 BC
The Abrahamic Covenant

c. 1440-1400 BC
The Wilderness Wandering

The Divided Kingdom

The Giving of the Law

c. 1010-970 BC
King David's Life

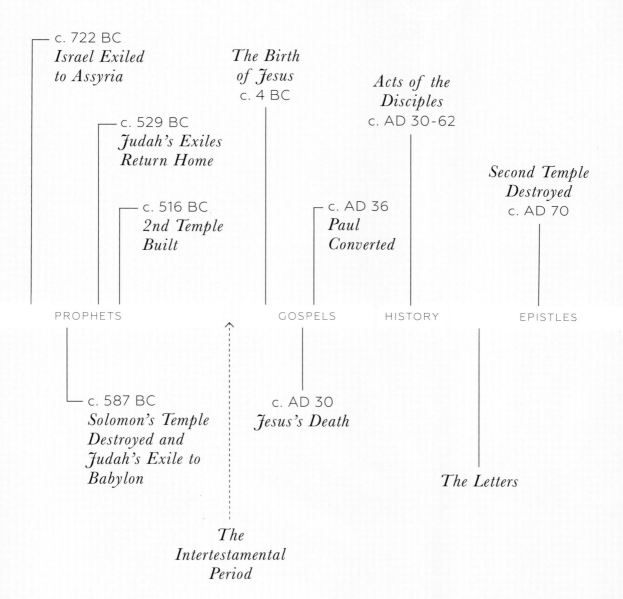

c. 722 BC
*Israel Exiled
to Assyria*

c. 529 BC
*Judah's Exiles
Return Home*

c. 516 BC
*2nd Temple
Built*

*The Birth
of Jesus*
c. 4 BC

*Acts of the
Disciples*
c. AD 30-62

*Second Temple
Destroyed*
c. AD 70

c. AD 36
*Paul
Converted*

PROPHETS

GOSPELS

HISTORY

EPISTLES

c. 587 BC
*Solomon's Temple
Destroyed and
Judah's Exile to
Babylon*

c. AD 30
Jesus's Death

The Letters

*The
Intertestamental
Period*

CONTENTS

REMAIN ROOTED IN GRACE

THE GOSPEL IS ENOUGH

READ GALATIANS 1-6

To add to the gospel is to lose the gospel. From beginning to end, the book of Galatians bursts with the power of the gospel of grace. We celebrate the truth that we are justified by faith alone, but believers can inadvertently add to the gospel by requiring adherence to unbiblical requirements to be in good standing with God. We can benefit from the corrections provided in Galatians. Paul's affirmation of the sufficiency of the gospel is a necessary rebuke for anyone who thinks that salvation requires more than faith in Christ who paid for our sins on the cross. The message of Galatians soothes the troubled consciences of those who fear they must do more to be saved. This letter exhorts us to remain rooted in grace alone through faith alone in Christ alone.

The Apostle Paul wrote Galatians. Previously known as Saul, he was converted on the road to Damascus while on his way to persecute Christians. His life was forever changed when Jesus appeared to him, calling him out of his life as a Pharisee and violent defender of Judaism. Like Paul, leaders of the Jewish religion rejected Jesus as the Messiah who promised to rescue God's chosen people, Israel. They continued to observe the laws and practices of the old covenant, rejecting the truth that Jesus kept the law perfectly, died to atone for sins, and was raised again. The Jews should have recognized Jesus as the Promised One of the Old Testament and should have been a light to the Gentiles, including them in the family of God. But many missed it and held tightly to Judaism. Paul was one of those people until the road to Damascus. Roughly fifteen years after his conversion, Paul wrote Galatians to a group of churches he had visited on his first missionary journey when he preached the gospel to them.

Galatia was located in the southern part of a Roman province, which is now part of modern-day Turkey. Rather than one ethnic group of people, the Galatian churches were made up of all sorts of believers, both Jews and Gentiles. When Paul visited Galatia on his first missionary journey, he stopped at the towns of Lystra, Pisidian Antioch, Iconium, and Derbe. After his trip, the churches in these towns were infiltrated by false teachers called Judaizers who argued that circumcision was necessary for salvation. These religious Jews tried to sway new Christians to continue upholding the law and submit themselves to circumcision, practices God had commanded under the old covenant, which was fulfilled in the coming of Christ. These practices were not necessary for salvation, but the Judaizers taught that they were. Though Paul had preached the gospel of Christ and justification by faith to the Galatians on his first trip, the Galatians quickly turned from the gospel of grace when pressured by the Judaizers. Paul's letter to them is both a rebuke for adding to the gospel and a celebration of what Christ had already done at the cross to fulfill God's law and free them from sin.

There is some debate about the date of the book of Galatians. The issue of circumcision and salvation was settled by the church fathers at the Jerusalem council in AD 49. Because Paul offers a strong correction in response to the false teaching of the Judaizers but does not mention the council in Galatians, it is likely that the letter predates the council and was written in early AD 49. Galatians was the first letter that Paul wrote and was one of the first penned books of the New Testament.

Galatians is an epistle—a letter that was meant to be read and circulated among the churches in that area. Like most of Paul's letters, Galatians opens with a greeting wherein the author identifies himself. However, unlike the rest of Paul's letters where he wrote about his love for the recipients, in Galatians Paul immediately moves to the body of his letter. He begins with a rebuke and defends his position as an apostle, something the Judaizers and others were refuting. He affirms the true gospel of Christ, underscores justification by faith alone, explains the reason for the law, describes the believers'

role as sons of God, celebrates freedom in Christ, and defines what it means to walk in the Spirit rather than the flesh. Running throughout most of the letter is an emphasis on the freedom believers have because of the finished work of Christ, not man. We obey God as a response to what has been done for us, and we do so in the power of the Holy Spirit, not the efforts of the flesh.

Paul's tone in Galatians feels incredulous. Why would anyone who has been freed from slavery willfully submit themselves to slavery again? Contemporary believers are unlikely to believe that we must be circumcised to be saved, but we are all tempted to add to the gospel of Jesus at times. Though our debt of sin has been paid by Jesus on the cross, we might be tempted to strive to do things for God to make sure we are tipping the scales of indebtedness in our favor. Though Scripture teaches that nothing can separate believers from His love, we might obey Him for fear that He will love us less when we miss the mark of holiness. Though we are justified by grace through faith in Christ alone, we might be tempted to keep a list of extra, good things we must do to maintain our good standing with God. Galatians provides us with the truth that there is only one gospel and one way to be saved: faith in Christ Jesus, who gave Himself for our sins to rescue us.

With the knowledge that we have been set free from sin and the law by Jesus's perfect life, death, and resurrection, we can now walk in complete freedom. Paul tells us that we do not have to yoke ourselves to extra practices to earn God's favor, but neither do we use His grace as a license to give ourselves to sinful behaviors. In Christ, we are free to live by grace through faith just as we were saved by grace through faith. The gospel is enough!

WE ARE FREE TO LIVE BY GRACE THROUGH FAITH JUST AS WE WERE SAVED BY GRACE THROUGH FAITH.

As you read the book of Galatians, note any key themes, words, or concepts, and mark them below.

Summarize the message of the book of Galatians.

Write a prayer confessing the ways you might have tried to earn God's favor, and ask Him to help you remain rooted in the sufficiency of Jesus's work at the cross for you.

GRACE AND PEACE

A GOSPEL GREETING

READ GALATIANS 1:1-5

The book of Galatians begins with its author. While this practice may seem odd to contemporary readers, the immediate identification of authorship was normal for the first century. Paul calls himself an apostle in verse 1, which is something he often did in his letters, but the significance of this identifying term would not have been lost on the Galatian readers. As we will see later in chapter 1, Paul's apostleship was in question by some, thus making it easy to undermine his teaching. Paul's immediate identification as an apostle "not from men or by man" is a clear rebuttal to this thinking.

"Apostle" means "one who is sent out," like a messenger representing someone else. While the generic term sometimes referred to those in missionary roles, like Barnabas or Titus, the specific title of an apostle was reserved for those who were commissioned by Jesus Himself to teach, preach, and lead the church. The original twelve disciples, minus Judas the betrayer, were called apostles. Because Paul came to faith when he encountered Jesus on the road to Damascus, he legitimately qualified as an apostle. And it was this encounter with the resurrected Jesus that changed his life.

Paul embeds the gospel into his greeting right away and anchors his apostleship in the commendation of "Jesus Christ and God the Father who raised Him from the dead" (Galatians 1:1). In the very first verse of the letter, Paul points the readers' eyes to Jesus the Messiah, who was raised from the dead by God the Father. Right away, Paul proclaims Jesus's death and resurrection. He pauses to include those with him in his greeting, which might refer to believers in Syrian Antioch, a possible location for the penning of this letter.

Paul then moves to the recipients of his letter, the Galatians. Paul visited these believers in the towns of Lystra, Pisidian Antioch, Iconium, and Derbe on his first missionary journey, which is documented in Acts 13-14. He shared the gospel with them on that trip and planted the churches. He knew these believers, and he wanted them to remain rooted in the truth of the gospel of Jesus. His letter to them is full of concern for their souls, and though he will rebuke them at times, his correction comes from a place of love and concern for their souls.

Grace and peace are the underpinnings of Paul's salutation. He could offer a greeting like this because he experienced the power of forgiveness and redemption through faith in Christ. This is the good news of the gospel that Paul will so strongly uphold throughout the book of Galatians: Jesus willingly gave Himself on behalf of our sins, according to God's will. Jesus the Son and God the Father were never at odds about this plan. It was the Father's will and the Son's willing obedience that culminated in Jesus's death on a cross to pay for our sins.

Both the original and contemporary readers should see the love and grace of God in this gospel-soaked greeting. We know real grace and peace when we come to faith in Christ, and we know real grace and peace when we continue in faith in Christ. Note Paul's use of the phrase, "to rescue us from this present evil age," in verse 4. We are saved from a life given to sin and destruction when the Lord gives us new hearts, but we are also being saved from sin continually as we grow in holiness and become more and more like Jesus. We still live in the present evil age, and we can see the effects of sin and death. Though we might look at the world around us and feel tempted to believe that evil will win, the Lord has delivered us from its grip, and He will fully deliver us when we are with Him in heaven.

Paul closes his greeting with a short doxology which is a song of praise to the Lord. He attributes all glory to God forever and ever. And God does deserve all the glory, for as Paul has summarized in his gospel greeting, the Lord has done all the work to save us, free us, and make us new. We cannot add to such a gospel when the work of salvation has been done by God through Christ. We, too, can worship the God who deserves all our praise.

> WE KNOW REAL GRACE AND PEACE WHEN WE COME TO FAITH IN CHRIST. AND WE KNOW REAL GRACE AND PEACE WHEN WE CONTINUE IN FAITH IN CHRIST.

Paul's greeting is full of gospel truth. What is the significance of his inclusion of the death and resurrection of Jesus in his salutation?

How does the knowledge that both God the Father and Jesus the Son are invested in your salvation impact your daily life? Does it make you feel secure in your standing before God?

What do you notice about man's involvement in salvation from this passage? How does this influence any temptation you might have to add to the gospel?

GOD'S FREE GIFT OF GRACE

NO OTHER GOSPEL

READ GALATIANS 1:6-10

In nearly all of Paul's other letters, he moves directly from greeting to gratitude, commending his recipients for the ways they faithfully followed Christ or upheld Paul in his ministry. Though Paul shows his affection for the Galatian Christians throughout his letter, he skips the customary commendation section by going directly to a rebuke. Paul is so far from gratitude that he has moved to astonishment. He is so amazed by how quickly the Galatians have turned from the true gospel that it merits a swift rebuke as soon as he can get the salutation out of the way. Paul's surprise at the speediness of the Galatians' turning away from the gospel he taught them seems to communicate that his visit to them was rather recent. This letter is quick on the heels of the news of their internal troubles.

Before we move to the impetus for their defection, we must note that Paul uses the present tense to describe what they are doing: turning. Buried in that verb is a bit of good news to celebrate before diving into the bad. The Galatians were presently in the process of turning away from the gospel when Paul wrote to them, which means that there was still time for them to be corrected and shift their gaze back to the true gospel of Jesus. James, the half-brother of Jesus, tells us that whoever turns back a believer from wandering away from the truth saves his soul from death and covers a multitude of sins (James 5:19-20). This is precisely what Paul is doing. His love and concern for the Galatians translate into a swift rebuke to warn them to get back onto the path of truth. He is concerned that in trying to enhance or change the gospel, they will lose it altogether.

Paul's language in today's passage does not point to mere passive neglect of the gospel. Rather, it illustrates a changing of sides, or of someone becoming a turncoat or traitor. We will see later that in adding to the requirements for salvation, the Galatians had moved from justification by faith alone to justification by faith and circumcision and adherence to the law. Whenever we add works to the gift of grace God has bestowed upon us in sending Jesus to pay for our sins, we lose the concept of grace. We reject God's gift and attempt to earn salvation ourselves, which we will never be able to do. When we try adding to grace, we lose grace. And when we lose grace, we lose God. The Galatians were changing sides, moving from the true gospel of grace to a gospel of works, though Paul is quick to clarify that a gospel of works is no gospel at all.

The word "gospel" means "good news." In pointing out the Galatians' embrace of a different gospel, he explains that there is no other good news for man beyond the message of Jesus, who gave Himself up for us to pay for our sins. It is not good news if we have to work or earn our salvation, thus, we cannot actually call those additions the gospel. In saying the Galatians were turning to a different gospel, he explains that it was not actually the gospel they were turning to. There were people within the Galatian churches troubling them and distorting the purity of the gospel of grace, drawing the Galatians' attention away from the gift of God and to the works of the flesh. Paul will write in a later letter to the Ephesian Christians that grace is a gift from God that prevents us from taking credit for our salvation (Ephesians 2:8-9). This is not a secondary or tertiary issue; the gospel is always primary. When we accept extra requirements for salvation, we reject God's free gift of grace.

We will find out later that these troublemakers within the Galatian churches were Judaizers bent on bringing circumcision and observance of the law into Christianity, but Paul takes their perversion of the good news of Jesus quite seriously. He calls for anyone, himself included, who teaches a different message of salvation, other than the gospel, to be cursed. The Greek term he used for "curse" is *anáthema*, which means "set aside for destruction or condemned to hell." Indeed, it is a dangerous thing to believe a false gospel, but how serious to teach it! Paul says that if anyone, whether himself or even an angel from heaven, preaches something beyond salvation by grace through faith in Christ alone, they should be condemned to hell. Other world religions have twisted truths from Scripture and adapted them for their worldview. Mormonism, for example, is a religion supposedly revealed by angels and teaches a different gospel from Scripture. Any purported gospel other than that of faith in Jesus Christ alone is dangerous to our souls. Belief in any other path for salvation will ultimately lead to death, and Paul was rightly concerned that the Galatians were heading down that path.

To prove that he is not overreacting in a childish outburst, Paul repeats himself in verse 9. So serious is his warning to the Galatians that he says it twice, calling those who distort the gospel anathema. Paul is aware that others have called him a people-pleaser and are questioning his grasp of the gospel, so he makes it abundantly clear in verse 10 that his concern for the Galatians is sincere because he is striving to please God alone. If he was more concerned with pleasing them, he would not have written such a strong letter of rebuke.

Paul's concern for the souls of the Galatians is merited, and we should be concerned for others who might be straying from gospel truth. We must keep our own souls in check by regularly turning our gaze to the pure, good news of salvation through faith alone in Christ alone. We cannot add anything to God's free gift of grace.

WHEN WE TRY ADDING TO GRACE.

WE LOSE GRACE.

What are some ways you are tempted to add to the gospel and thus lose it, today?

Read 1 Timothy 1:3-7. Why must we correct erroneous teaching within the church? How can we do this with kindness and love?

What is the measuring stick for good news? How can we differentiate between the true gospel and other religious teachings of the world?

FROM ANGRY PERSECUTOR TO
JOYFUL PREACHER

WHAT THE GOSPEL CAN DO

READ GALATIANS 1:11-17, ACTS 22:6-21, ACTS 26:4-23

On the heels of Paul's swift correction of the Galatians' turning from the gospel is the beginning of his defense of the gospel he had been preaching. Those stirring up trouble in the Galatian churches were criticizing his position as an apostle and calling into question the validity of his gospel message. Paul's response is testimonial in nature. He calls the readers back to his life prior to salvation before showing how God's grace has been manifested in his life as a preacher of the good news of Christ. But first, he explains where he received the gospel in the first place.

The New Testament apostles were those who received the message of salvation from Jesus Himself. Since Paul's conversion occurred after Jesus's death and resurrection, the criticism about his apostleship might seem valid at first. Paul's reply to this criticism includes three rebuttals to the claim that he came up with his gospel message himself. First, in verse 11, he says that the gospel he preaches is not of human origin. In verse 12, he follows up with two more statements to prove his point. He did not receive the gospel from a human source. He received it by the revelation of Jesus. Neither his mission nor his message was from Paul himself; both were from God. To underscore his argument, Paul beckons the Galatians to remember who he was before Christ gave him the gospel.

Personal testimony can be a helpful method for sharing the gospel, and this is precisely what Paul utilizes to prove he could never have come up with the message of salvation through faith in Jesus. Paul defends his apostleship and the gospel message through the three stages of his testimony that serve as an example we can follow when sharing our faith with others. Paul explains who he was before salvation, what happened when God saved him, and what his life has been like since his salvation. Sharing a personal testimony of the Lord's grace in our lives as Paul does here can help others see what the gospel can do for anyone who believes in Jesus.

No one with Paul's background would make up a message of salvation through Jesus. In fact, he was fanatically against that message before God saved him.

Though Paul had likely told the Galatians about his past when he visited them, they probably already knew. Before encountering Jesus, Paul was a known persecutor of Christians. And Paul makes it abundantly clear that persecuting the church was not enough for him. He "tried to destroy it" (Galatians 1:13). Additionally, he was zealous for the traditions of his fathers and advanced in Judaism beyond his peers. He was a Pharisee, highly ranked among the religious leaders, and full of malice toward those who believed that Jesus was the promised Messiah the Jews were waiting for. The book of Acts fills in other details about Paul's background, noting that he would enter house after house, drag off men and women who were Christians, and imprison them. He "was convinced that it was necessary to do many things in opposition to the name of Jesus of Nazareth" (Acts 26:9). More than that, he approved of the death sentences those saints received. Paul was not just indifferent to the gospel message—he was antagonistic toward it. According to Acts 26, he would go into the synagogues where believers gathered and attempt to force them to blaspheme the name of Jesus. He was "terribly enraged at them" (Acts 26:11) and pursued them to foreign cities—exactly what he was doing when God intervened.

The book of Acts provides three accounts of Paul's encounter with Jesus. In each one, Paul is confronted by a blinding light while on a road to Damascus where he planned to persecute the church. A voice addresses Paul, calling out his Hebrew name, Saul, asking, "Why are you persecuting me?" The voice belonged to Jesus, who appoints Paul as a servant and commissions him to take the message of salvation to the Gentiles, that they would believe and receive forgiveness for sins. It is for this purpose that Jesus has confronted Paul, and as Paul explains in Galatians 1:15, it was always God's plan.

Moving to the next portion of his testimony, Paul explains to the Galatians what God has done for him. The emphasis shifts from Paul's actions to God's actions. It was God who set Paul apart from before birth, not only to believe in Jesus but to become an ambassador for Christ to the Gentiles, those outside the Jewish faith and ethnicity. By His grace, God called Paul and was pleased to reveal Jesus to him. This revelation was not only life-altering for Paul, but it was the foundation of the gospel he preached. He did not yet travel to Jerusalem to hear the gospel from the apostles. He did not consult with others to borrow their messages and adapt them to his own. His revelation of Christ was authentic and true and was later validated by those who had walked with Jesus Himself.

From angry persecutor to joyful preacher, from devout Pharisee to devoted missionary, from proud zealot to humble servant—this is what the gospel of Jesus did for Paul, and this is what the gospel of Jesus can do for everyone who believes in Him alone for salvation.

SHARING A PERSONAL TESTIMONY OF THE LORD'S GRACE IN OUR LIVES AS PAUL DOES HERE CAN HELP OTHERS SEE WHAT THE GOSPEL CAN DO FOR ANYONE WHO BELIEVES IN JESUS.

Read Acts 8:1-3 and 9:1-20. What do you notice about Paul before his encounter with Jesus? How might his testimony have helped the Galatians see that he was not preaching a man-made gospel but rather a God-given one?

_____

_____

_____

_____

_____

Read Acts 22:6-21 and 26:12-18. Why do you think Jesus asked Paul, "Why are you persecuting me?" when Paul was traveling to arrest Christians and have them imprisoned and killed?

_____

_____

_____

_____

_____

If you are a believer, write out a short testimony of your faith in Christ, using the pattern that Paul used in today's passage. Share who you were before faith in Christ, how you came to faith in Christ, and what your life has been like since then. If you are not a believer, what does Paul's transformation teach you about the power of the gospel?

_____

_____

_____

_____

_____

_____

PRAISE GOD FOR MAKING
YOU NEW

A TRUSTWORTHY MESSAGE

READ GALATIANS 1:18-24

Whenever we listen to a preacher or teacher, we tend to trust the message more if we know the speaker personally. If we know the person to be full of integrity, humility, and love for Christ, we will trust that what he or she is teaching us is true and right. If you cannot trust the messenger though, you are unlikely to trust the message. Paul's dilemma with the Galatians was that they knew him, but the Judaizers who were stirring up trouble in the churches made them question if Paul was really an apostle and if the message he preached was trustworthy. If the Galatians did not trust him, then they were unlikely to listen to his corrections. Paul seeks to set the record straight by briefly outlining the fourteen years of his life after his conversion to prove that he is who he says he is and that his gospel came directly from God, not man.

The Judaizers apparently accused Paul of borrowing the original apostles' gospel message and adapting it to his own. But geographically, this claim was impossible. The apostles were in Jerusalem. Paul was converted on a road to Damascus—some 135 miles from Jerusalem—where he spent three years alone, preaching in the synagogues. He said in Galatians 1:18 that after those three years of preaching alone, he went to Jerusalem to meet Peter, known as Cephas. Paul also met James, Jesus's half-brother, and stayed only fifteen days in Jerusalem. That was not enough time for Paul to receive the whole counsel of God from Peter or James. This was a quick trip where Paul spent much of his time preaching the gospel and conversing with the Hellenistic Jews who tried to have him killed. The apostles sent Paul to Tarsus, his hometown, which is in the region of Cilicia. Paul's story is consistent with Luke's account in Acts 9, confirming that Paul was telling the truth about his whereabouts. He had alibis. He was not hiding out in Jerusalem listening to Peter or James tell him the whole story of Jesus. He did not have to because He already knew the story of Jesus from Jesus Himself.

Paul pauses in his timeline to comment on the churches in Jerusalem. Though they had not yet met him personally, they heard what happened to him on that road to

Damascus. They kept hearing that "he who formerly persecuted us now preaches the faith he once tried to destroy" (Galatians 1:23). This is a miraculous turn in Paul's story. Paul had switched sides completely. He became an ambassador of the very message he once tried to destroy. He was not just a passive representative but someone who would suffer greatly for the gospel he used to hate. Acts 9:19-25 provides insight into Paul's three years in Damascus. He was preaching the gospel and being persecuted for it. The Jews in Damascus conspired to kill Paul, and he had to escape with the help of his friends. The one who rounded up Christians to imprison them and send them to their deaths was now the object of similar persecution. This Paul is a messenger who believes his message with all of his heart.

Paul's defense of his apostleship and true gospel message continues in chapter 2 as he picks up his timeline and travelog again to show that the message he received from Jesus was the same message the other apostles received from Jesus. His goal is to help the Galatians see that they can trust the message of salvation through faith in Christ alone that he had taught them on his previous visit. He tells his story to garner their trust so that they would receive his correction and turn back to the true gospel. But Paul is not quite finished talking about his past.

At the end of chapter 1, Paul speaks of the Jerusalem Christians and their response to his salvation story. He says that "they glorified God because of [him]" (Galatians 1:24). Whenever we hear a story of someone's faith in Jesus, we should respond with worship. God alone can take an enemy of the gospel and make him an ambassador of the gospel. God alone can transform a devoted persecutor of Christians into someone who would gladly endure persecution for the sake of the Savior he once hated. That is miraculous! Only God can take dead hearts and make them beat for Him. Only God can move us from the kingdom of darkness into the kingdom of light. Only God can redeem our sinful souls and mold us into the image of His Son.

The right response to the salvation story of a believer in Jesus is worship. When you think about your own story of faith in Christ, you can rejoice that you are not who you were. You can praise God for making you new. He is committed to conforming you to be like Christ. He works in our lives today as He did in Paul's life. It might not look as dramatic as Paul's conversion story, but it is always a miracle.

ONLY GOD CAN TAKE DEAD HEARTS AND MAKE THEM BEAT FOR HIM. ONLY GOD CAN MOVE US FROM THE KINGDOM OF DARKNESS INTO THE KINGDOM OF LIGHT. ONLY GOD CAN REDEEM OUR SINFUL SOULS AND MOLD US INTO THE IMAGE OF HIS SON.

Read 2 Corinthians 11:24-33. Paul mentions some of the sufferings he endured, including his narrow escape from Damascus. Contrast this passage with what you know of Paul before the Lord saved him.

Read Romans 8:18, part of a letter by Paul. What helped Paul, who used to hate the gospel of Jesus, remain devoted to it even while being persecuted?

Write out a prayer, thanking God for miraculously saving you. List some of the ways you see that He continues to work in your life to make you like Jesus.

PAUL'S ALIBI

GALATIANS 1:18-19

Then after three years I did go up to Jerusalem to get to know Cephas, and I stayed with him fifteen days. But I didn't see any of the other apostles except James, the Lord's brother.

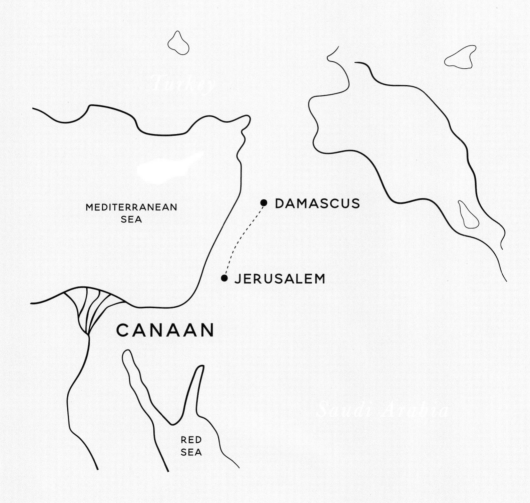

FROM JERUSALEM TO DAMASCUS:
Approximately 135 miles
45 hours at normal walking pace

Turkey

MEDITERRANEAN
SEA

● DAMASCUS

● JERUSALEM

CANAAN

RED
SEA

Saudi Arabia

GRACE TO YOU AND PEACE
FROM GOD THE FATHER AND
OUR LORD JESUS CHRIST,
WHO GAVE HIMSELF FOR OUR
SINS TO RESCUE US FROM
THIS PRESENT EVIL AGE,
ACCORDING TO THE WILL OF
OUR GOD AND FATHER.

—

GALATIANS 1:3-4

WEEKLY REFLECTION

REVIEW GALATIANS 1:1-24

Paraphrase the passage from this week.

What did you observe from this week's text about God and His character?

What does this week's passage reveal about the condition of mankind and yourself?

How does this passage point to the gospel?

How should you respond to this passage? What specific action steps can you take this week to apply this passage?

Write a prayer in response to your study of God's Word. Adore God for who He is, confess sins that He has revealed in your own life, ask Him to empower you to walk in obedience, and pray for anyone who came to mind as you studied.

WE ARE ABRAHAM'S OFFSPRING
BECAUSE WE SHARE HIS FAITH

A GOSPEL AGREEMENT

READ GALATIANS 2:1-10

Eleven years passed between Paul's first and second trips to Jerusalem. In Galatians 2:1, Paul picks up his travelog with his second trip to visit the apostles. He mentions in verse 2 that the impetus for his trip was "a revelation," meaning that God sent him to Jerusalem. In Acts 11:27-30, a prophet named Agabus from Jerusalem traveled to Antioch and predicted a severe famine in the Roman world. As a result, the believers in Antioch pooled their resources to send relief to Jerusalem. The emissaries sent to Jerusalem with the love offering were Paul and Barnabus.

The monetary relief was not Paul's only business in Jerusalem though. He went to present the gospel he had received from Christ and preached for more than a decade to the apostles, namely James (Jesus's half-brother), Peter (known as Cephas), and John. Though Paul was sure of the gospel message, he wanted to be certain that the Jerusalem apostles were not undermining his ministry behind his back. The Judaizers infiltrating the churches were standing by their motto: "Unless you are circumcised according to the custom of Moses, you cannot be saved" (Acts 15:1). If James, Peter, and John supported the Judaizers' circumcision creed, then Paul would not be able to partner in ministry with them.

Originally, circumcision was a good thing commanded by God to set apart His people from the rest of the pagan world. According to the covenant God made with Abraham in Genesis 17, any male belonging to God's people would be circumcised as a sign of God's covenant to multiply His people and bless them through the family of Abraham. They would bear on their bodies a reminder of God's faithfulness to keep His covenant. To be clear, circumcision did not save God's people. The saints of the Old Testament, like Abraham and Moses, were saved by grace through faith, according to Hebrews 11:39. Circumcision was a sign that they were part of God's covenant community.

Ultimately, the Abrahamic covenant was fulfilled in Jesus who kept the law perfectly and was the one through whom all peoples of the earth would be blessed, including Gentiles. Because His righteousness is imputed, or attributed, to all who believe, we are freed from the confines of the law. Under the new covenant, we are brought into God's family through faith in Christ, not circumcision. We are Abraham's offspring because we share his faith. It was fine for the Jews to be circumcised after the coming of Christ as long as they did not make it a requirement for salvation. Yet, that is exactly what the Judaizers were doing: forcing Gentile Christians to become Jews first.

Paul's companions on this trip were interesting choices. He took with him Barnabas, a Jewish Christian, and Titus, a Greek Christian. Titus, in particular, became a believer because of Paul's mission to the Gentiles. He also was uncircumcised. Taking such a man to stand before the Jerusalem apostles was risky. Would they pressure Titus to become circumcised to be a full-fledged Christian? Paul answers in verse 3, "But not even Titus, who was with me, was compelled to be circumcised, even though he was a Greek." Paul accuses the Judaizers of infiltrating the church and spying on their Christian freedom in an attempt to enslave believers to the practice of circumcision. The result of any addition to the gospel is a loss of Christian freedom. The very point of the free gift of grace from God is that it is free. We cannot earn it, and when we try to do more to earn God's favor, we lose the concept of grace altogether, thus shackling ourselves to meaningless traditions and works. Whatever we add to the gospel, to that we will be enslaved.

The apostles, though ordinary men like Paul, had an important influence. If they agreed with the Judaizers, then Paul's ministry would have been fruitless. The apostles did not agree with the Judaizers, however. On the contrary, they affirmed Paul's gospel message of faith alone by grace alone in Christ alone and supported his mission to the Gentiles while they focused primarily on preaching the gospel to the Jews. The apostles' agreement with Paul is significant in that the message of faith alone in Christ alone continues to be the foundation for salvation, a doctrine on which we firmly stand today. Remember, the gospel is not good news for us if it requires us to work our way to God.

Titus, then, was not compelled to do anything else to follow Jesus. He came to salvation the same way the apostles had: through faith in Christ. And that was enough. Titus went on to become a prominent figure in the early church, eventually pastoring the church on the island of Crete. Paul's ministry to the Gentiles was in partnership with the other apostles' ministry to the Jews. Between the two groups, the gospel spread like wildfire throughout the earth. Your faith in Christ today is in part a result of this partnership!

The trip to Jerusalem was fruitful for Paul. The apostles backed his ministry and the gospel message, validating his position in his letter to the Galatians who doubted him. He had the apostles' backing on the issue of circumcision as well, which would come up again and be settled for good at the Jerusalem Council a few years later. Additionally, the apostles agreed with Paul that in their ministries to Jews and Gentiles, they should remember to care for the poor. James, who was present at this meeting, urges us to practice true religion by caring for widows and orphans (James 1:27). The result of saving faith in Christ is good works. Paul had come to this meeting with a love offering for the Jerusalem Christians; he was eager to continue this care, and as the church grew, so too did the care for the poor Christians in the churches.

UNDER THE NEW COVENANT, WE ARE BROUGHT INTO GOD'S FAMILY THROUGH FAITH IN CHRIST.

Circumcision is not an issue in the church today, but there are other good things that we might try to attach to salvation by grace through faith in Christ. List any practices or traditions that you view as necessary to be a believer?

In verse 5, Paul says that they did not submit to the false teaching of the Judaizers "so that the truth of the gospel would be preserved for you." How does his firm stance on grace alone through faith alone in Christ alone impact your faith today?

Titus was a living example of Paul's ministry to the Gentiles. Read Titus 1:1-4. How does the gospel unite people of different ethnicities and people groups?

Read 2 Corinthians 8:1-6. The Macedonian Christians were noted for giving "beyond their ability" to other believers when they themselves were poor. How does a gospel of grace encourage care for the poor?

GOSPEL-ROOTED LIVING

AN APOSTLE'S REBUKE

READ GALATIANS 2:11-14

Belief in the gospel should result in gospel-rooted living, but sometimes the fear of man trumps our fear of God, and we act in ways that contradict what we believe to be true. Paul had a word for this kind of double-mindedness: hypocrisy. The word "hypocrisy" in Galatians 2:13 is *hypokrisis* and was used in the context of the Greek theater. The actors in ancient Greek plays wore large masks to cover their faces and were called hypocrites, meaning that they put on another persona and played parts that were not truly theirs. We all know hypocrisy when we see it, but few of us dare to correct another believer the way Paul did when he saw Peter's two-faced playacting in Antioch.

After recounting his trip to Jerusalem where he addressed the issue of circumcision and salvation with James, Peter, and John, Paul shares with the Galatians another story to highlight the damage that comes from adding to the gospel. Paul was in the city of Antioch, a very diverse city where the church was made up mostly of Gentiles. It was in Antioch that followers of Jesus were first called Christians, and the city served as a home base for Paul. He likely wrote Galatians while in Antioch. After Paul's second trip to Jerusalem, Peter paid him a visit to Antioch. Peter made himself at home there, sharing a table with the Gentile Christians, just as he would with family. In ancient times, table fellowship was more than just sharing a meal. Eating together demonstrated approval and acceptance of one another. And this was a big deal for Jews and Gentiles.

Under the old covenant, to protect them from their inclination to worship pagan gods, Jews were commanded not to mingle with Gentiles. Dietary laws kept the Jews from eating unclean foods, which also set them apart from the world. Relations between Jews and Gentiles were usually tense. Jesus was often criticized by the Jewish religious leaders for mingling with Gentiles because the Pharisees deemed His presence among them as unclean. Jesus said, though, that He came not to abolish the law but to fulfill it (Matthew 5:17). The laws were never intended to be permanent practices for God's people. Rather, they were meant to set them apart from pagan nations and point them to their coming Savior, Jesus, who obeyed the law perfectly and took the punishment of sin for us. Because of His work, we are no longer bound by the law, including the food laws. Christians did not need to isolate themselves from the world the way Israel once did because the family of God was no longer restricted to a political-ethnic group. The family of God would be made up of believers from all people groups and would live by the Spirit, not the law.

However, the Apostle Peter, like many Jewish Christians, kept following Israel's customs regarding food and fellowship—that is, until God sent him a vision that changed everything. Acts 10 tells the story of Peter's vision wherein God declared all foods clean before sending Peter to share the gospel with a Gentile named Cornelius. Peter would not have made the trip to enter a Gentile's home had it not been for the Lord's vision, for doing so would render him ceremonially unclean according to the law. But in Christ, Peter was free from the ceremonial law. The vision helped him to see that. Cornelius was saved after Peter shared the gospel with him and received the gift of the Holy Spirit just as the Jewish Christians had. Peter said in Acts 11:17, "If, then, God gave [the Gentiles] the same gift that He also gave to us when we believed in the Lord Jesus Christ, how could I possibly hinder God?" Peter became convinced that Gentile Christians were saved just as Jewish Christians: by grace through faith in Christ. They were united and equal in Christ. That belief was evidenced by his willingness to eat and fellowship at the table with the Gentile Christians of Antioch.

But that changed when the Apostle James and some Jewish Christians visited Antioch. James's companions were believers in Christ, but they still held to the practice of Judaizing the Gentiles—that is, circumcising Gentiles and requiring them to follow the law. Essentially, the Judaizers believed that Gentiles should become Jewish in order to be full-fledged Christians. Again, we see that the Judaizers added requirements to the gospel that God does not. Nowhere does God require us to follow Jewish customs and laws to be saved. His qualification is faith in Christ and nothing more.

Peter knew this and believed it, but he cracked under the pressure of the visiting Judaizers who would

have deemed his fellowship with uncircumcised Christians unclean. He stopped eating with the Gentiles, withdrawing from them altogether. He was not living what he believed about the gospel and instead succumbed to his fear of man. His hypocrisy was not personal only to him; it affected those around him—so much so that even Barnabas was led astray by Peter's actions. And what about the Gentile Christians who had enjoyed Peter's fellowship? What did Peter's withdrawal communicate to them? Were they second-class Christians because they had not been circumcised?

Paul vehemently defends the salvation of the Gentile Christians—and no wonder! He has been fighting for the purity of the gospel for years, especially regarding circumcision. He confronts Peter to his face in front of everyone, calling out his hypocrisy for what it was. Peter's sin was public and influenced other Christians to follow suit. Paul's correction must be public as well. Paul was not disparaging Peter or his position as an apostle. He was simply defending the truth of the gospel from which Peter and those who followed his example were deviating. Any Christian can slip into sin; none of us are above what Peter did. We all need correction at times. When the truth of the gospel is at stake, correction might be sharp, but it is necessary and loving.

Paul's appeal to the Galatians thus far has been one of those sharp but loving corrections. The Galatians were erring the same way the Judaizers and Peter had. Adding something like circumcision as a requirement for salvation drove a wedge between an already divided group of people. But there are no second-class Christians. We all come to faith the same way: by grace alone through faith alone in Christ alone. Jesus unites us despite our differences, and it is unity in Him that will outlast all other earthly attempts at reconciliation. If we require Christians to uphold a standard that God does not, we are hypocrites in danger of losing the gospel of grace.

Read Acts 10. Summarize Peter's vision and his visit to Cornelius. What was the outcome?

Paul's public correction of Peter is sharp but necessary. Read 1 Timothy 5:20-21. Why is loving correction a good thing within the church?

Read James 2:1-13. Can you think of any historical examples of favoritism or extra-biblical requirements for salvation within the church? List them below, and explain why they were not in agreement with Scripture.

Read 1 Peter 1:1-2 and 2:1-10. Peter wrote this letter to suffering Gentile Christians years after his hypocritical behavior in Antioch. How did God change Peter's thoughts and actions toward Gentile believers?

WE GET TO CLAIM HIS
RIGHTEOUSNESS

JUSTIFIED BY FAITH

READ GALATIANS 2:15-21

Woven throughout the final verses of Galatians 2 is Paul's explanation of what we call the doctrine of justification. Today's passage is not a mere compilation of theological treatises. No, the doctrine of justification is paramount to our foundational understanding of salvation. What we learn about our reconciliation with God in Galatians 2:15-21 should put to rest any human attempts at earning favor or right standing with Him.

To be justified is to be declared righteous before God. Justification is a legal term that illustrates the exchange made at the cross wherein Jesus, who knew no sin, became sin and bore the curse of death in our place (2 Corinthians 5:21). When we believe in His atoning sacrifice for sins, His righteousness is imputed, or attributed, to our account. The debt against us has been paid in full. Because Jesus paid for our sin, we get to claim His righteousness as our own. Rather than owing a debt of sin, we are credited with the holiness of Jesus!

Since the garden of Eden, man has tried to make his own way to God. We think we can be good or moral enough to tilt the scales in our favor. But even if we kept the entire law of God, failing in only one little point, the Bible teaches that we are guilty of breaking the whole law (James 2:10). We can never do enough good things to tilt righteousness our way because even our best deeds are tainted with sin (Isaiah 64:6). We are helplessly unable to fix our sin problem. And in God's grace and kindness, we do not have to. The only way we can be declared righteous is by faith in Jesus, but this is not a restrictive doctrine. No, it is incredibly freeing. We are free from fruitlessly trying to save ourselves. Justification by faith alone squashes our attempts at self-salvation and enables us to embrace God's free gift of grace.

Continuing his defense of the true gospel, Paul explains that every Christian comes to salvation in the same way—by faith in Christ. Jews must be justified by faith in Christ. Gentiles must be justified by faith in Christ. There is no other way to be declared righteous. Paul says it three times in verse 16, widening the reach each time. First, he says that "a person is not justified by the works of the law but by faith in Jesus Christ." So generally speaking, we cannot be justified by adherence to God's commands under the old covenant; we must be justified by faith in Jesus. Second, he explains that "we might be justified by faith in Christ and not by the works of the law," meaning that personally he, Peter, and his readers must be justified by faith alone in Christ. And third, he makes a universal application, saying that "by the works of the law no human being will be justified." Including all people both generally and specifically, Paul shows there is no exception. Everyone must be justified by faith to be saved.

The gospel levels the ground beneath our feet. We all come to Jesus the same way—through faith in Him and nothing more. As the old hymn "Rock of Ages" states, "Nothing in my hand I bring, simply to Thy cross I cling." We all come with nothing. We all must depend wholly on Jesus's sacrifice for our right standing before God. This is the crux of Paul's argument with the Judaizers regarding circumcision or keeping the dietary laws of the old covenant. Adherence to those things cannot declare us righteous before God. Only faith in Christ declares us righteous before God. Therefore, we cannot require those who have been justified by faith in Christ to take additional steps to be reconciled to God. In Christ, they are already justified. Paul knew it was fruitless and antithetical to the gospel to require the Gentile believers to do anything more than believe in Jesus. If keeping the law blamelessly would have saved anyone, Paul would know. But as he shared in his own testimony, it got him nowhere. He needed Christ to make him new.

Paul must have felt an argument coming because he then launches into a defense of Christian freedom. Perhaps the Judaizers had argued that not keeping the law would always result in immoral living. If the requirements of the law are loosened or removed, surely Christians would run headlong into sin. "Absolutely not!" Paul exclaims. Living freely in Christ does not promote a sinful lifestyle—it cannot. Justification by faith in Christ is completely at odds with a pursuit of sinful living. Paul explains why in verses 19-20.

"For through the law I died to the law, so that I might live for God," Paul says. Jesus is the only one who kept the law perfectly. He died, thus satisfying the law's demands for death as payment for sin. And in His death, we who believe die, too. Our pasts are blotted out, our sins are paid for, the debt is canceled against us. But it does not end there. We now live by faith in Christ who lives in us. Those who have been justified by faith are not who they used to be. Though they still struggle with sin, they are no longer marked by a lifestyle of sin because they no longer live for themselves. They live for Christ and through Christ. Remember Paul's former life? Remember him after meeting Jesus? True saving faith does not produce a love for sin.

If we could achieve salvation on our own, then Jesus's sacrifice would have been for nothing. Trying to add to our right standing before God by calling attention to good works or extra requirements is to say that Jesus's death was not enough for us. But in God's remarkable grace, Jesus's death is all we need to be declared righteous. Justification by faith in Christ is good news for us because it is enough for us.

WE ARE HELPLESSLY UNABLE TO FIX OUR SIN PROBLEM. AND IN GOD'S GRACE AND KINDNESS, WE DO NOT HAVE TO.

In your own words, define justification by faith. List some ways you may have tried to justify yourself before God. How is your definition of justification at odds with that list?

In verse 20, Paul brings justification by faith very close to home. Focusing on the last phrase of that verse, how should we view our salvation in Christ personally?

Read 2 Corinthians 5:17-20 and Ephesians 4:20-24. How do we continue to "live by faith in the Son of God," knowing that we are declared righteous but still struggle with sin?

WE WILL NEVER DEPART FROM OUR
NEED TO SEE CHRIST CRUCIFIED

SANCTIFIED BY FAITH

READ GALATIANS 3:1-5

Perhaps you have never struggled with the doctrine of justification before. Maybe you have no trouble agreeing that you are saved only by grace through faith in Jesus Christ. But have you ever wondered about what comes next? Sanctification is the process of becoming more and more like Jesus, and it begins the moment we believe the gospel and are justified by faith in Christ. But somewhere along the way, we might get the idea that while we are justified by faith, we are sanctified by effort. Have you ever felt that your life in Christ after salvation depends solely on your obedience and attempts at being good enough to be called a Christian? In today's passage, we will see how Paul's second rebuke of the Galatians proves that the entire Christian life is lived by faith rather than works.

If you think Paul's rebuke in 1:6 is harsh, then brace yourself. He begins chapter 3 by addressing the "foolish Galatians!" His astonishment at their abandoning of gospel truth rises to the surface in a rapid succession of rhetorical questions. Through these questions, Paul draws the Galatians' attention to what they already knew to be true to help them see where they had erred. We all need a continual reminder of the gospel to shed light on areas where we have disbelieved God or leaned toward a particular area of sin. Correction is a gift!

Paul's questions get to the heart of the issue quickly. Surprised by their bent toward the Judaizers' false teaching, he wonders if they had been bewitched. It is true enough that Satan works to turn our hearts away from the gospel. As in the Judaizers' claims, our enemy can convince us to add good things to the gospel, undermining Jesus's finished, perfect sacrifice on the cross. It might not seem like such a terrible thing to make good, religious traditions a requirement for salvation, but it nullifies the need for Jesus to have died for us. As we have learned, to add to the gospel is to lose the gospel.

The Galatians, like us, did not witness Jesus's life, death, and resurrection personally, but when they heard the gospel preached to them, they could picture Christ being crucified the same way your mind creates pictures when you hear a story (Galatians 3:1). Paul tells us in Romans 10:17 that "faith comes from what is heard, and what is heard comes through the message about Christ." Hearing the gospel is necessary for salvation. In hearing or reading the message of Jesus, we, in a sense, see Him crucified and risen. The Galatians heard this very message from Paul himself, and they believed it. That was all that was necessary for them to be saved—faith alone. Paul knows that they knew this, so he presses them further. Did they receive the Holy Spirit when they believed the gospel or when they began obeying the works of the law? Again, they know the answer. They received the Spirit when they believed, just as the other first-century Christians did (Acts 10:44-47, 11:18), and just as all Christians do (Romans 8:9, Galatians 4:6).

The Spirit gave them the gift of faith and had been at work among them, resulting in changed lives. It was evident that they now belonged to Christ. So in light of the fact that the Galatians were saved and received the Spirit when they heard and believed the gospel, Paul asks a question in verse 3 that we all must consider. "After beginning by the Spirit, are you now finishing by the flesh?" Even if you grew up in church, you may struggle with the answer to this question. Because of our human tendency to work for our right standing and approval, many Christians will assent to justification by faith while living like they are sanctified by works. Yet, our sanctification is as dependent upon the work of the Spirit as our justification was. Though life in Christ is lived in obedience to His commands, we cannot in any way obey in our own strength. We cannot finish what the Spirit began. We will never live the Christian life disconnected from the work of the Spirit. We need the gospel for salvation, and we need the gospel for sanctification. We will never depart from our need to "see" Christ crucified.

Buried in all of Paul's questions to the Galatians is the foundational truth that just as we are justified by faith, so are we sanctified by faith. We were dependent upon the Spirit's work to impart faith so that we could believe the gospel, and we are daily dependent upon the Spirit's work to help us live this new life in Christ and through Him. We will always live the Christian life by faith in the One who loves us and gave Himself up for us.

WE WERE DEPENDENT UPON THE SPIRIT'S WORK TO IMPART FAITH SO THAT WE COULD BELIEVE THE GOSPEL, AND WE ARE DAILY DEPENDENT UPON THE SPIRIT'S WORK TO HELP US LIVE THIS NEW LIFE IN CHRIST AND THROUGH HIM.

In verse 4, Paul alludes to the fact that the Galatians had suffered for their faith in Jesus. Why would their suffering be for nothing if they continue to require circumcision or adherence to the law as necessary to salvation?

Read Philippians 2:12-13 and Colossians 2:6-7. How do these verses (also written by Paul) support today's passage on sanctification by faith?

Write down some of the ways you have tried to work out your sanctification without the Spirit's help or involvement. Confess those to the Lord in prayer, asking Him to help you continue in the Spirit rather than the flesh.

JUSTIFICATION BY FAITH

ABRAHAM'S FAITH

READ GALATIANS 3:6-9

Hundreds of years before Paul wrote his letter to the Galatians, God promised a childless man named Abraham that He would bless all the people of the earth through his family. In Genesis 12, God promised Abraham, "I will make you into a great nation, I will bless you, I will make your name great, and you will be a blessing...and all the peoples on earth will be blessed through you." This was not just a promise to give a barren couple a longed-for child. This was a promise to send a Savior to atone for the sin of people from every tribe, tongue, and nation.

The Jews knew Abraham as the patriarch of Judaism—a founding father, so to speak. It was from his family line that the people of Israel came. The Jews, and particularly the Judaizers who thought the Gentile Christians should adopt Jewish customs, esteemed Abraham as a paramount fixture of their faith. God had made a covenant with Abraham in Genesis 17, requiring Abraham and every male in his household to be circumcised. Because of this, the Judaizers believed that for one to belong to God, one had to belong to Abraham, and to belong to Abraham meant being circumcised. But there was a hole in their argument.

Paul draws the Galatians' attention to the timing of God's covenant and Abraham's response. God came to Abraham, not the other way around. God made His promises to Abraham while he was still an uncircumcised outsider living in a pagan land. God made promises to Abraham about blessing the world through his offspring, which he did not yet have. God did all of this in his kindness and grace. The timing is important: before he was circumcised, Abraham believed God, and according to Genesis 15:6, God "credited it to him as righteousness." Abraham did obey God, but before he obeyed, he believed. And it was his faith in God that counted as righteousness. Back in Genesis, justification was still accomplished by faith.

So what does this mean for the Galatians? It means that they were accepted on the same basis that Abraham was—by faith. The Judaizers tried to require circumcision by bringing up Abraham, but Paul demolished their argument using the very person they did. Circumcision did not make Abraham right before God.

Faith did. Circumcision does not make you Abraham's sons. Faith does.

Abraham had never heard the name of Jesus, but he believed God and trusted Him to provide atonement for his sins. We see an example of his faith in Genesis 22, when God tested Abraham by telling him to sacrifice his only son, Isaac. This was the same child God had promised to Abraham decades before. This was the child through whom all the people of the earth would be blessed, and God told Abraham to sacrifice him on an altar. Abraham obeyed, even when his son asked him where the sacrificial lamb was as they traveled to the location of the intended sacrifice. Abraham replied, "God himself will provide the lamb for the burnt offering, my son" (Genesis 22:8). Abraham obeyed because he trusted God would provide. Hebrews 11:19 helps us see how Abraham's faith was demonstrated. "[Abraham] considered God to be able even to raise someone from the dead; therefore, he received [Isaac] back, figuratively speaking." Abraham believed God could resurrect Isaac to keep His promise, if necessary. God intervened, and Abraham did not have to sacrifice his son. Instead, God provided a ram for Abraham and Isaac to sacrifice instead. Abraham believed God would provide a sacrifice, and He did.

Paul says in verse 9 that "those who have faith are blessed with Abraham, who had faith." We are called to trust God for a sacrifice for sin just as Abraham did. We are blessed in that we know the name of the sacrificial Lamb provided for our sins—Jesus. Abraham was blessed with a son and a life of obedience to the God who called him, but his greatest blessing was his justification by faith. That is the greatest blessing we can receive too. Through Abraham's family came a baby born in Bethlehem. Jesus was a Jew whose lineage is traced back to Abraham, and it is through Jesus that we are saved. The promise of blessing for the whole world was fulfilled in Jesus. Any person from any ethnic background can be forgiven, saved, and reconciled to God through faith in Jesus Christ. You do not have to be Jewish, you do not have to be circumcised, and you do not have to observe the works of the law to be Abraham's sons. You only need faith in Christ.

Justification by faith has always been God's plan. It was His plan for the Galatian Christians, and it is His plan for Christians today. The Judaizers might have tried to use Abraham's story as a way to put Gentile Christians in slavery to the works of the law, but Abraham's story points us to the free gift of grace that comes through justification by faith alone in Christ alone. If we must become Abraham's sons to belong to God, then we must have faith as he did. It is not genetics or adherence to the law that makes us the sons of Abraham. It is faith. That is all that God requires. The gospel is good news for us because it comes to us through faith and nothing else. And that has been God's good plan from the beginning.

ABRAHAM DID OBEY GOD.
BUT BEFORE HE OBEYED, HE BELIEVED.
AND IT WAS HIS FAITH IN GOD THAT
COUNTED AS RIGHTEOUSNESS.

Read Romans 4:1-12. What do you notice in verse 12 about the timing of Abraham's obedience to be circumcised? How does this passage support Paul's appeal to the Galatians in 3:6-9?

Read Matthew 1:1-17. In your own words, explain how Jesus was the fulfillment of God's promise to bless all the people on earth through Abraham.

Have you believed in Jesus for the forgiveness of your sins? If so, write out a prayer, thanking God for providing Jesus as the lamb for your sacrifice. If not, reflect on what may be keeping you from believing that Jesus is enough to pay for your sins.

I HAVE BEEN CRUCIFIED
WITH CHRIST. AND I NO
LONGER LIVE. BUT CHRIST
LIVES IN ME. THE LIFE I NOW
LIVE IN THE BODY. I LIVE BY
FAITH IN THE SON OF GOD.
WHO LOVED ME AND GAVE
HIMSELF FOR ME.

—

GALATIANS 2:20

WEEKLY REFLECTION

Paraphrase the passage from this week.

What did you observe from this week's text about God and His character?

What does this week's passage reveal about the condition of mankind and yourself?

How does this passage point to the gospel?

How should you respond to this passage? What specific action steps can you take this week to apply this passage?

Write a prayer in response to your study of God's Word. Adore God for who He is, confess sins that He has revealed in your own life, ask Him to empower you to walk in obedience, and pray for anyone who came to mind as you studied.

JESUS TRADED PLACES WITH US

THE RIGHTEOUS WILL LIVE BY FAITH

READ GALATIANS 3:10-14

When was the last time you sinned? An hour ago? A minute? It might have been a sharply spoken word, a jealous thought, a selfish action, or a deliberate indulgence in something displeasing to God. Sin is disobedience to God, and ever since Eden, it has permeated every part of our lives. We are all guilty of missing the mark of God's holiness (Romans 3:23). Our sin is not just an inconvenience. It separates us from God, damning us to an eternity in hell. Stained as we are by our rebellion against God, we are unable to fix our plight and make ourselves right before Him. The payment for sin is death (Romans 6:23). Paul's letter to the Galatians does not deny our helpless state. In chapter 3, Paul helps us see why trying to keep God's law (or even the contemporary equivalent of living moral lives) will never undo the curse we bear for sinning against God.

According to Paul's explanation of faith and works in Galatians 3, it is theoretically possible to be justified by keeping God's law—that is, if anyone could actually keep the law. That is the problem Paul points out. It is not possible. No one can keep God's law perfectly; therefore, no one can be justified by the works of the law. Our sinfulness makes it a dead end. Those who cannot obey God's law perfectly bear a curse for their sinfulness. That means that except for Jesus, every human who has ever lived or will live is under a curse because no human can obey God perfectly. If being declared righteous before God depends upon our perfect law-keeping, then we are all doomed.

So what was God's point in giving a law to His people that they cannot keep? It was to reveal sin and point us all to the One who could obey perfectly and redeem us with His own blood.

God's law was given to Moses and the Israelites after God delivered them from slavery in Egypt. God gave very specific commands to the people to keep them separate from the pagan nations all around them. He told them to "keep [His] statutes and ordinances; a person will live if he does them" (Leviticus 18:5). But, they did not do them. They disobeyed constantly. There was no way for Israel to live by the law because their sin was a continuous problem. But, as Paul points out in Galatians 3:11, the righteous do not live by the law. They live by faith! Just as we are declared righteous by faith alone in Christ alone, we find life—eternal life with God—by faith alone in Christ alone. We do not have to die for our sins as the payment demands because Jesus stepped in to fix our desperate problem.

Jesus obeyed God's law perfectly and lived completely without sin—the only one to ever do so. He was not cursed in any way. Yet, He did something astonishing—"Christ redeemed us from the curse of the law by becoming a curse for us" (Galatians 3:13). Jesus traded places with us. Perfect, holy, sinless Jesus suffered the curse of sin by becoming the curse for us in our place. He never sinned, yet He became sin—our sin—and died on a cross to pay for it. The wages of sin is death, and Jesus paid the debt for those who believe in Him. He endured the suffering we deserve and gave His life for ours. It is an exchange like no other. He took our wretched sin upon Himself and gave us His pure righteousness. He did this in a shameful, humiliating way—hanging on a tree like a heinous criminal.

God said in Deuteronomy 21:22-23 that when "anyone is found guilty of an offense deserving the death penalty and is executed...anyone hung on a tree is under God's curse." The Jews would have objected greatly to a Messiah crucified on a cross. Historians equate the Roman method of execution to being hung from a tree; crosses were made from crude beams of wood from trees. Why would the Savior sent from God be sentenced to die a criminal's death? Here is why the gospel is good news for us: we are the criminals. We are the ones who deserve the death sentence on a tree. It was our curse Jesus took on Himself when He died on the cross. He was cursed for us. And He swallowed every bit of God's righteous wrath in our place. This is grace. It is not something we could ever attain for ourselves.

Through Jesus's payment for our sins with His own life, we have been freed from the curse of the law and the sentence of death. But that is not all. We have been freed to receive all the blessings of God through Christ. When we believe in Jesus's atoning sacrifice for sin, we receive the gift of the Holy Spirit who enables us to live by faith, grow in godliness, and persevere until we see God face-to-face. We will enjoy a perfect, sinless life with God in heaven forever. This is what Jesus has given us in trading places with us. We could never do it ourselves, and that, according to Paul, is entirely the point. We live by faith in Christ Jesus, not by works. From beginning to end, the Christian life is always lived by faith.

THROUGH JESUS'S PAYMENT FOR OUR SINS WITH HIS OWN LIFE, WE HAVE BEEN FREED FROM THE CURSE OF THE LAW AND THE SENTENCE OF DEATH.

Have you believed in Jesus's payment for your sin, or are you still under the curse?

Read Romans 4:16-25. Paraphrase Galatians 3:14 in light of that passage.

Read 2 Corinthians 5:21. Write out a prayer thanking Christ for trading places with you at the cross, becoming a curse for you, and making you righteous. If you are not a believer, write out a prayer asking God to help you understand and believe what Jesus did at the cross.

week 3 day 1 / 65

THE GOSPEL REALLY IS
GOOD NEWS FOR US

CHRIST'S BLESSINGS ARE OURS

READ GALATIANS 3:15-18

About five centuries before God gave the law to Moses for the Israelites, He made His covenant promises to Abraham. To Abraham, He made promises, and to Moses, He gave the law. His promises to Abraham required nothing of Abraham but faith. The law He gave to Moses required obedience that the Israelites could not supply. Why did He give both promises and the law? Are His ways with Abraham at odds with His ways with Moses and the Israelites? We might read today's passage and wonder which one He expects of us: faith or works?

The Galatians were likely wondering the same thing after being thoroughly confused by the Judaizers who tried to marry the law of Moses with the promise of Abraham. Faith was not quite enough to the Judaizers, so they added strict adherence to the law as a requirement for salvation. The Galatians probably heard their arguments and wondered as we do. Why would God give the law and demand obedience if He credited Abraham with righteousness for believing Him? Paul answers our questions by using a nearly universal illustration — a last will and testament.

Even in ancient times and in various cultures, wills were handled much the way they are now. Once the owner of the will passed away, the contents of the will could not be changed or revoked. Whatever gifts promised to the named beneficiary had to be given. Much the way things are done now, the beneficiary of a will did not have to perform tasks for the owner of the will. Rather, the beneficiary simply received what was promised. God's promise to Abraham did not include a list of laws Abraham had to obey or tasks he had to complete to obtain God's promises. In His covenant, God put all the action on Himself. He promised to give Abraham an innumerable number of descendants. He promised to bless the whole world through Abraham's family. He promised to lead Abraham to the land He would give him. Abraham simply had to believe that God would keep His promises, and when he did, God credited it to him as righteousness.

Long before God gave the law to Moses, He freely and graciously made those promises to Abraham. If obeying the law was necessary to be declared righteous, then Abraham had no chance. He lived nearly 500 years before the law was given! He could not obey a law that had not yet been given. But because justification comes through faith, not works of the law, God was just to declare Abraham righteous based only on faith. Paul's continued argument for justification by faith is solid, but he is not done yet.

God's promises to Abraham did not end with Abraham. They were meant for His offspring, and specifically, Paul points out, to one person from Abraham's family — Jesus. God's promise to Abraham was ultimately for Christ. He is the main beneficiary and recipient of God's promises. Why is that good news for us? We have learned that in the great exchange that happened at the cross, Jesus became our sin and took our curse upon Himself. He traded places with us and paid for our sins with His own blood. When we believe in His perfect, sinless sacrifice for our sins, He imputes, or attributes, all of His righteousness and holiness to us. We get to claim it as our own because, in Him, it is our own. We are unified with Christ, and we live all of our lives in Him. Remember Paul's words from chapter 2: "I have been crucified with Christ, and I no longer live, but Christ lives in me. The life I now live in the body, I live by faith in the Son of God, who loved me and gave himself for me" (Galatians 2:20). When we are justified by faith in Christ, we receive all of His blessings. We can even say that all He has is ours. We are co-heirs with Him (Romans 8:16-17). That means we get to share His inheritance. So all of God's promises of blessing that He made to Abraham were ultimately made to Abraham's seed, meaning Jesus. And if they were made to Jesus, then those who have believed in Him for the forgiveness of sins get to share in the benefits of those promises. The gospel really is good news for us!

God did not negate or undo His covenant with Abraham when He gave the law 500 years later. He did not change His mind or decide that faith was not enough. He did not give the law to seal up the cracks where faith was insufficient for justification. No, He still justified His people by faith alone when He gave the law to Israel. His promises and His law are not at odds. As we will see tomorrow, His law illuminates His promises, showing us how glorious the benefits of His covenant are for us in Christ.

WHEN WE BELIEVE IN HIS PERFECT, SINLESS SACRIFICE FOR OUR SINS, HE IMPUTES, OR ATTRIBUTES, ALL OF HIS RIGHTEOUSNESS AND HOLINESS TO US.

Note Paul's use of "brothers and sisters" in verse 15 to address the Galatians. If, in Christ, there is no partiality between Jew and Gentile, what does that also mean for men and women?

_____

_____

_____

_____

_____

Read Romans 8:16-17 and Colossians 3:9-11. How does being in Christ affect our daily living? How does it affect the way we relate to one another within the church?

_____

_____

_____

_____

_____

According to verse 16, the main beneficiary of God's promises to Abraham is Christ. How is that good news for us?

_____

_____

_____

_____

_____

GOD'S LAW WAS GIVEN FOR
THE SAKE OF SINS

THE PURPOSE OF THE LAW

READ GALATIANS 3:19-26

If the law could not make Abraham, Moses, or any of God's people righteous, why did God give it? Paul asks and answers this question succinctly in verse 19. "Why then was the law given? It was added for the sake of transgressions until the Seed to whom the promise was made would come." Note the words "added" and "transgressions." The law was not given to cancel out God's promises to Abraham. Instead it was added until God would fulfill those promises by sending Christ. The law was added because of transgressions, or sins, against a holy God.

Laws and rules do not make us good, perfect people. Rather, they help us see the difference between right and wrong, revealing where we have failed to do what is right. In our context, societal laws help us to function within a civil code that serves to protect people and, to an extent, restrain evil. Similarly, God's law was given for the sake of sins. It provided boundaries that would protect Israel from running headlong into pagan worship like the nations around them, a very real temptation to which they gave themselves over and over again. The law provided a way for the people to make sacrifices to temporarily atone for their sins and to know how to address others who sinned against them. The law set them apart from the world around them, marking them as those who belonged to God. And as they struggled to keep it, the law revealed to them how desperately they needed lasting atonement for their sin. The law has never made anyone righteous, but it has always revealed man's need for righteousness.

One notable difference between the law God gave to Israel and the promises He made to Abraham was in the way He gave them. He spoke His promises directly to Abraham, but He gave the law through Moses and—as Paul mentions—angels, meaning that the law was given through mediators as the law passed from God to angels to Moses to Israel (Deuteronomy 33:2, Acts 7:53). Paul is not denigrating the law. Rather, he is showing that the law served the promise and prepared the way for the gospel. The law is not contrary to God's promise, Paul exclaims. If it had been able to give life, then righteousness would be attainable through the law. But as we have learned, no one can keep the law perfectly, besides Christ, so no one can become righteous through the law. That was never the point of the law.

Paul says that the law served as a prison warden, so to speak, to guard God's people until the time was right to send Jesus. In this sense, the law was like a strict prison guard, keeping God's people from trying to find justification elsewhere until it was readily and fully available through faith in Jesus Christ who died to pay for sins. Once Jesus came, we did not need the guardian anymore. God's law might seem harsh to us, but there is great mercy in God giving it, for without the law we would not know how much we need Christ.

Paul says that "the knowledge of sin comes through the law" (Romans 3:20) and that he "would not have known sin if it were not for the law" (Romans 7:7). He explains that through the law, we know what God expects of us. We see our failure to produce that kind of holiness, and we discover that we are desperately unable to fix our sin problem. This is a merciful gift from God because when we finally realize that we cannot make ourselves right before God, we can see how good the good news of the gospel is for us. We need to grasp the bad news first—that we are desperately wicked and in need of a Savior—so that we can believe and rejoice in the good news that Jesus came to save wicked sin-ners and reconcile them to God. Once we recognize our sinful state, we can find hope in the Savior sent to pay for our sins at the cross and free us from guilt and shame.

The law, then, is not in opposition to God's promise of salvation. Rather, the law leads us to the promise. They work together. The law convicts us of sin, shows us we need a savior, and points us to Christ. Then, when we believe Christ for the atonement for our sins, we receive all of Christ's blessings and promises that God made to Abraham.

Once Christ came, the requirements of the law were completed through His obedience. Working in conjunction with God's promises, we can see that the law was a good plan. It was a temporary plan, but it was a good plan. Human beings are good at taking something created for good and twisting it to be used for ill. The Judaizers did this with God's law, hanging it over the head of Galatian believers who did not come from the Jewish background. But, as Paul explains repeatedly, there is no need for us to adhere to God's laws in order to be saved. While we do obey the commands of Christ to grow in godliness and to love one another, we do not require things like circumcision or adherence to dietary laws as part of the salvation process. Both the law and the promise together help us see that our justification is by faith alone in Christ alone.

WITHOUT THE LAW WE WOULD NOT KNOW HOW MUCH WE NEED CHRIST.

Though Gentiles were not given God's law like the Israelites were, we are still imprisoned by the law until we believe in Jesus's perfect sacrifice as payment for our sin. Read Romans 2:14-15. How were Gentiles held captive to guilt under the law before coming to faith in Christ?

Read Romans 5:18-21. How does the law lead us to grace?

Why is it necessary for us to see our sinful state before God before finding hope in Jesus's sacrifice for sins?

A BRAND NEW FAMILY

WE ARE ONE IN CHRIST

READ GALATIANS 3:27-29

Much of our striving and struggles in life stem from our desire to belong to something or someone. We long to feel secure in our relationships. We yearn for our lives to have meaning. We want to know and be known. One of the sweet gifts of the gospel of grace is that when we believe in Christ and His sacrifice for our sins, we are granted the ultimate place of belonging with all the meaning and security we could hope for. Our salvation experience does not end with justification by faith. That is only the beginning. In Christ, we have a brand new family and a brand new identity.

Paul's encouragement to the Galatians at the end of chapter 3 is one of welcome and confidence. Not only do Gentile Christians not have to adopt Jewish traditions or old covenant works to be followers of Christ, but they share the same status as children of God with the Jewish Christians. In Christ, we are all equal. More than that, we are family. Paul speaks of our identity in Christ and what that means for how we relate to one another as Christians.

Paul begins by saying that those "who were baptized into Christ have been clothed with Christ." Baptism is a sacrament of the church — a signifier of grace that has been received from God. It represents that believers have been washed clean of their sins and are walking in the newness of life in Christ. Baptism does not save anyone, and Paul certainly was not implying that it does. He goes to such great effort to prove that salvation comes only by faith in Christ, he would not add baptism as a requirement for salvation. However, baptism signifies that we have died with Christ and now live in Him (Galatians 2:20, Romans 6:3-5). Baptism is an outward response to an inward change that has occurred. We respond to the gospel with obedience by publicly professing that one has come to faith in Christ and has received the Holy Spirit, who dwells in every believer.

What does it mean to be "clothed with Christ"? In Paul's time, there were a couple of occasions that were signified by donning new garments. One was when a child passed into manhood and received his full rights as heir. As we will see in Galatians 4, a child could be named heir but did not have any rights to the inheritance until he or she reached a certain age. Once that age, the child put on new garments to signify the changed status from child to heir. Similarly, a slave could be adopted by his master, and on that occasion, the slave would put on new, white garments to note the change in his status. So it is with believers. When we come to faith in Christ, we are transferred from the domain of darkness to the kingdom of Jesus (Colossians 1:13). We, who were far off, have been brought near to Christ (Ephesians 2:13). Our status has changed from rebellious enemies of God to beloved children of God. This status change is true of every person who believes in Christ, regardless of race, rank, or gender.

Throughout all of history, man has treated his fellow humans with partiality. Racism, sexism, and classism still permeate our societies, influencing the way we treat others depending upon their skin color, gender, or socioeconomic background. This is as true today as it was in Paul's day. Paul pushed against the social norms and declares the equality we all share as brothers and sisters in Christ. Though we do not diminish or deny our skin color, gender, or socioeconomic background, we do not allow those differences to drive a wedge between us. We can celebrate our differences while holding fast to the deeper and stronger source of our unity, which is Jesus Christ. As Christians, we belong first and foremost to Him. Our other descriptors come second to our identity in Jesus Christ.

In Paul's day, to be a female or a slave would have made you one of the lowest-ranked individuals in society. If you were Jewish, you would add being a non-Jew to that list. Paul shows us in verse 28, though, that being "in Christ" obliterated the entire sinful ranking system since "you are all one in Christ Jesus." Belonging to Christ means inheriting His blessings that were promised to Abraham. Therefore, if you belong to Christ, you belong to Abraham and share in Christ's inheritance. No matter your skin color, gender, or socioeconomic background, you are on equal footing with every other believer. Christ unites us, making us all siblings who have the same Father. There is no caste or class system in Christ. We are heirs of the same promise as Abraham, which means we stand in a long line of saints who believed God and were credited with righteousness. We can read the names of the people in Hebrews 11 and call them family. We can read of Paul, the Galatian Christians, and the churches in Rome, Ephesus, and Antioch and identify with our brothers and sisters who lived and died by faith before us.

Because we are heirs with Christ, one day we will worship God in heaven, standing around His throne with people from every nation, tribe, people, and language (Revelation 5:9). We will worship together with our spiritual family forever because Christ has united us and made us part of God's forever family.

WE CAN CELEBRATE OUR DIFFERENCES WHILE HOLDING FAST TO THE DEEPER AND STRONGER SOURCE OF OUR UNITY, WHICH IS JESUS CHRIST.

DAILY QUESTIONS

How does the gospel of Jesus provide us a place of permanent belonging?

Read Ephesians 2:11-22 and Revelation 5:9-10 and 7:9-10. How does Christ unite people from different backgrounds? What is our guarantee that He will unite us with believers who are different from us?

How do you see partiality in your own heart? Are you uncomfortable fellowshipping with particular groups of people or even certain personality types?

WE HAVE EVERYTHING WE NEED
TO FOLLOW CHRIST FAITHFULLY

IF SONS, THEN HEIRS

READ GALATIANS 4:1-7

In ancient Jewish culture, a child could be named as the heir of an estate, but as long as he was a child, he had no rights to his inheritance. In name, he might be the owner of everything in his father's house, but in actuality, he had no more access to it than a slave might have. He was disciplined by trustees and tutors who guarded him until he was old enough to inherit it. Once he matured into manhood, he became the heir in both name and possession. He no longer needed guardians but had full access and rights as the heir to his father's estate.

Paul uses this analogy to compare the state of man under the law with the state of man in Christ. God gave His people the law to prepare them for the gospel. Like a child had to grow up and wait until the time was right to inherit and receive his full rights as son and heir, God's people had to wait for the right time when God sent His Son, Jesus, into the world to both free them from slavery under the law and to make them His sons. Using the analogy, it is as though God gave His people the law in childhood to prepare them for the gospel in adulthood (Galatians 3:24). Though Satan exploited the law and used it to enslave men, God meant for the law to prepare His people for the coming of Christ.

God sent Jesus at just the right time. In His sovereign wisdom and goodness, God prepared the world for the coming of Christ. Jesus was sent by God, signifying His divinity, and Jesus was born to a woman, signifying His humanity. He was born as a Jew under the law that only He would obey perfectly. Jesus was uniquely qualified to be our Savior, and God sent Him at the perfect time to a waiting world.

When Christ was born, much of the ancient world was under Roman rule, and although God's people were oppressed under Rome, the Romans built roads to connect the cities and countries they governed. Not only were God's people desperate for a deliverer from the law, but the gospel would have literal roads to travel after Jesus came, lived, died, and was raised. When Jesus sent out His followers to make more disciples in Matthew 28, there were concrete roads for them to travel as they shared the gospel message. Additionally, under Roman rule, Greek was the commonly spoken language, which made the gospel accessible without a language barrier. God was not just sending Jesus when things got tough. He had always planned to send Jesus at a specific time, and He did this not just to rescue His people but to make them His own children.

Paul says in verse 5 that Jesus came "to redeem those under the law." His redemption language alludes to the purchase of a slave's freedom. Slavery in ancient times was sometimes voluntary because of debt. That debt could be paid by a redeemer, thus freeing the slave. Jesus came to purchase our freedom from the law and slavery to sin. He paid the redemption price with His own life. But He did not just come to free us. He came to make us children of God. Paul says that Jesus came "so that we might receive adoption as sons." Our status has moved from rebellious enemies of God to beloved children of God. Then, as now, adoption changed the status of a person from outsider to family member. As binding as biological sonship, adoption makes it possible for an adoptee to receive the full rights and inheritance of a natural-born son. If you are a female reader, do not let the masculine language discourage you. Daughters could not inherit in ancient times, so when Paul calls us "sons," he is including women who believe in Jesus. Female believers will inherit fully as though natural-born sons of God. The doctrine of adoption changes everything for us! Though we were slaves to sin under the law, Jesus freed us to become sons of God who receive an inheritance—all the blessings of Christ that were promised to Abraham.

We see the full trinitarian Godhead at work in our justification and adoption. God sent Jesus into the world (Galatians 4:4), and He sent the Holy Spirit into our hearts (Galatians 4:6). Jesus came to make us sons in status, and the Holy Spirit came to ensure that we experience real sonship. The Spirit lives in our hearts, enabling us to cry out to the Father with intimacy. "Abba, Father" is like a child's desperate cry for the help and comfort of a father. Likewise, as adopted children of God, we have the right to experience an intimate relationship with God as a perfect, loving, kind Father.

All that is required for us to have this kind of close relationship with God is faith. When we believe in Jesus for the atonement of our sins, we are justified before God. We are made righteous and freed from sin under the law so that we can be adopted as sons into God's family. And if we are sons, we are heirs to the great inheritance that we share with Christ. From slave to son and heir, we can experience the extravagant love of God who sent Jesus to free us, save us, redeem us, and make us family. With our new identity and status, we have everything we need to follow Christ faithfully.

AS ADOPTED CHILDREN OF GOD, WE HAVE THE RIGHT TO EXPERIENCE AN INTIMATE RELATIONSHIP WITH GOD AS A PERFECT, LOVING, KIND FATHER.

What are some of the practical reasons that God sent Jesus "when the time came to completion," or at just the right time?

Read Ephesians 1:3-10. How has God shown His great love for us? List at least five ways that He expresses His love in this passage.

Do you enjoy intimacy with God? Do you think of Him as a Father who loves you? Based upon our text today, describe what you think intimacy with God looks like.

CHRIST REDEEMED US FROM
THE CURSE OF THE LAW BY
BECOMING A CURSE FOR US...

—

GALATIANS 3:13

REVIEW GALATIANS 3:10-4:7

Paraphrase the passage from this week.

What did you observe from this week's text about God and His character?

What does this week's passage reveal about the condition of mankind and yourself?

How does this passage point to the gospel?

How should you respond to this passage? What specific action steps can you take this week to apply this passage?

Write a prayer in response to your study of God's Word. Adore God for who He is, confess sins that He has revealed in your own life, ask Him to empower you to walk in obedience, and pray for anyone who came to mind as you studied.

A KIND FATHER

KNOWN BY GOD

READ GALATIANS 4:8-11

Imagine a man who was born into slavery. Throughout his childhood and early adult years, he lived as a slave, unable to do anything about his position. But one day, someone purchased his freedom for him, setting him free. Then, the slave was adopted by a kind father who gave him the full rights, inheritance, and standing of a natural-born son. The former slave was not only free but now a son of a father who loves him. But then one day, the man decided he preferred slavery over being a free son, so he sold himself back into slavery. We would question such a decision. Surely the man was not thinking correctly. Who would trade freedom and a relationship with a kind father for slavery? Yet, this is what the Galatians were doing, and this is the reason Paul wrote his letter of correction to them.

In Galatians 4:8-11, Paul contrasts who the Galatians used to be with who they are now in Christ. He has just explained spiritual adoption to them in verses 1-7, showing the rights and privileges that they have as sons of God. Before salvation through faith in Jesus Christ, the Galatians were slaves to what they worshiped. Since most of the Galatians were Gentiles, they came from pagan backgrounds, most likely worshiping Roman and Greek gods. They did not know God and were instead worshiping things that were not God and could never be God. They were enslaved to that fruitless idolatry until God saved them.

But now, Paul tells them they know God. And they only know Him because He first knew them and made them alive in Christ. It was always God's plan to save those who would belong to Him. Paul tells us that God "chose us in him, before the foundation of the world, to be holy and blameless in love before Him. He predestined us to be adopted as sons through Jesus Christ for Himself, according to the good pleasure of His will" (Ephesians 1:4-5). John tells us that we love God and others because He first loved us (1 John 4:19). To be saved and made new in Christ is to be loved and known by God. The Galatians were former pagan worshipers but were now known and loved by God since believing in Jesus for the atonement of their sins. They had been freed from the worship of false gods and slavery to sin. Their freedom came through faith in Christ.

And yet, the Galatians were returning to slavery once again by subjecting themselves to Jewish traditions and practices as requirements for salvation. Paul likens the practices of observing "special days, months, seasons, and years" (Galatians 4:10) to their former pagan worship. Though the Jewish traditions (like circumcision) were not sinful in and of themselves, they were optional. They were not to be added as requirements for salvation. Anything we add to justification by faith will enslave us. That can include good, spiritual things too. We can check off the boxes of Bible reading, prayer, and church attendance without truly loving and knowing God in the process. When we reduce discipleship to following rules and regulations, we enslave ourselves to useless worship and miss the intimacy of a relationship with God, our kind Father. Rather, as sons who enjoy a personal relationship with God, we obey Him out of love. We read our Bibles and pray and attend church to know Him more deeply, to enjoy His presence, and to grow in faith. Whenever we try to do those things to earn a better standing before God or to be more loved by Him, we are returning to slavery, forgetting that we are already loved by Him and forgetting that we have already been made righteous through Christ.

Why would anyone return to slavery? Paul asks the Galatians this question, wondering if his ministry to them was in vain. Paul's ministry was not just a checklist of people to write letters to or to visit now and then. He was deeply invested in the church in Galatia. He had spent time with them, teaching them about Jesus, showing them the futility of their pagan worship in light of the hope of the gospel. He prayed for them and cared for them. As we will see later in chapter 4, he pleads with the Galatians as a pastor who deeply cares for his congregation. He did not want to see them forsake their sonship, which was bought by the precious blood of Jesus, in exchange for hopeless, helpless slavery again. His fear that his ministry had been in vain was an appeal for them to hold on to the gospel for which he had labored and loved. He knew that the gospel was their only hope for true freedom.

When we have believed in Jesus for the atonement for our sins, we are moved from helpless slave to beloved son. We have the rights and inheritance of natural-born children, and we are loved and known by God. Faith is all that is required of us to become the children of God. As Paul shows us in today's passage, it is folly to reject the sonship that we receive by faith for slavery that can never free us.

TO BE SAVED AND MADE NEW IN CHRIST IS TO BE LOVED AND KNOWN BY GOD.

What are some things that you feel you must do to be loved by God? How are those things preventing you from enjoying intimacy with God?

Why do we read our Bibles, pray, and attend church? How do we make sure those things flow from our hearts as an obedient response to God's love rather than a motivation for God's love?

Read 1 Thessalonians 2:8-12. Describe Paul's ministry to those with whom he preached and shared the gospel.

COMMITTED TO THE TRUTH

SPEAKING THE TRUTH IS LOVE

READ GALATIANS 4:12-16

In today's cultural climate, tolerance is king. Letting people live as they deem right without judgment is supposed to communicate love and support. More than that, our society encourages us to celebrate whatever personal decision someone makes—no matter how detrimental it might be to their spiritual, physical, or mental health. To love is to live and let live. Yet, the Bible teaches something different. Love is patient and kind and forgiving, but it is also committed to the truth. Jesus's half-brother, James, wrote, "whoever turns a sinner from the error of his way will save his soul from death and cover a multitude of sins" (James 5:20). Love corrects error and is more concerned with the state of someone's soul than with their reputation. Paul exhibits this kind of love in his correction of the Galatians' theological error.

The first time Paul visited Galatia and shared the gospel with them, he came with considerable physical suffering. Some theologians suspect that Paul suffered from malaria or another wasting disease, but others think Paul had a degenerative eye condition. While we do not know for sure what his suffering included, the Galatians certainly did. Paul's presence with them was somewhat of an imposition, yet they received him—his physical maladies and his gospel message—with joy and care. Perhaps Paul was using hyperbole in Galatians 4:15, or maybe he was referring to an actual eye condition, but it is apparent from the passage that the Galatians did everything they could do to care for him in his fragile state. They recognized that he was preaching the gospel truth to them, and they welcomed both the message and the messenger.

In ancient Greece, people believed that illness or disease were signs that the pagan gods were displeased with a suffering individual. People avoided the sick or treated them poorly so as not to associate positively with them. The Galatians' care for Paul in his suffering, then, was extraordinary in light of the cultural views of illness. Paul praises them in his letter for their prior care for him. Yet as he is writing to correct their theological error of adding to the gospel, it seems as though they have shifted in their opinion of him. Where once they welcomed him with exemplary care, now they are turning their backs on him because they disagree with his message. Paul has not changed and neither has his message of faith alone in Christ alone, but the Galatians were changing in their stance on salvation after the Judaizers had influenced them. Once they found themselves in disagreement with Paul, their attitude toward him changed. Paul asks them plainly, "So then, have I become your enemy because I told you the truth?" (Galatians 4:16).

Speaking the truth in love can be received by others as a judgment or unwelcome criticism. We tend to demonize those we disagree with, turning on the messenger so we do not have to listen to the message. But when someone offers correction in our life, we should see it as an act of love, not judgment. With humility, we can examine the correction for biblical truth and pray for the Lord to help us see where we might need to repent of sinful living or unbiblical beliefs. Paul's correction of the Galatians is one of love. He is concerned for their souls. Their belief that salvation comes through something more than faith in Christ was an error that endangered their souls and their eternity. Paul's correction was born of genuine love and concern, and he longs for them to view it that way.

In verse 12, Paul begs the Galatians, "Become like me, for I also became like you." When Paul first came to them, he lived among them and spent time with them. Unlike Peter who waffled in his behav-ior among the Gentiles, Paul lived as they did. As he wrote it in another letter, he became "all things to all people, so that [he] may by every possible means save some" (1 Corinthians 9:22). In light of his willingness to assimilate into their culture to share the gospel with them, Paul pleads with them to become as he is—a Christian committed to the authentic gospel without any additions. Paul desires them to know the freedom that comes from believing in the atoning sacrifice of Jesus. He does not want them to be enslaved to anything else any longer. Paul's correction is an expression of love and concern for their souls. He is not their enemy; he is a beloved friend who cares deeply for them.

Paul suffered much in his life for the sake of the gospel. He was beaten and imprisoned multiple times. He had physical maladies that he prayed for God to remove. Yet he realized that Christ was magnified in his suffering, and for that reason, he could persevere in the work God called him to among the Gentiles. His weaknesses did not prevent him from his ministry but rather spurred him to depend on God's grace and strength. We can view our suffering the same way. God can, and often does, use all sorts of things in our lives to teach us to depend on Him. And as we persevere in following Christ, we can make much of His faithfulness to us in our conversations with our unsaved friends and family members. It might be through our weaknesses that we can speak the truth of the gospel in love to those around us who desperately need to hear it.

LOVE IS PATIENT AND KIND AND FORGIVING. BUT IT IS ALSO COMMITTED TO THE TRUTH.

Have you ever been on the receiving end of loving correction? How did you respond, and what did you learn from it?

Read 2 Corinthians 12:6-10. Why does Paul rejoice in the sufferings that the Lord did not remove from his life? How might God use your suffering for good?

What prevents you from speaking the truth of the gospel to others around you? Why is it unloving toward your neighbors, family members, or co-workers to keep the gospel to yourself?

WHEN WE COME TO FAITH IN
JESUS CHRIST, HE CHANGES US

SHAPED BY CHRIST

READ GALATIANS 4:17-20

When we come to faith in Jesus Christ, He changes us. He makes us new creatures who live for Him rather than for ourselves. Because the Holy Spirit now dwells in us, we put off our old ways and live our new lives in Christ (Ephesians 4:17-24). God begins to shape us into the image of His Son, Jesus, for our good and His glory. The longer we follow Christ, the more we look, think, and act like Him. As we grow in our knowledge of and love for Him, our hearts are shaped by Christ. This spiritual formation is what Paul desired for his dear Galatian Christians. As we have seen Paul both rebuke and correct the Galatians, we also see him yearn for their growth in Christ as a mother labors in love for the birth of her child.

Paul was not the only one fighting for the Galatians' affections, however. The Judaizers were working hard to win the Galatians over to their way of thinking. But Paul makes it clear that the Judaizers do not have the Galatians' best interests at heart. "They court you eagerly, but not for good," Paul says in verse 17. They want the Galatians to cut Paul out of their lives so that the Judaizers have sole influence over them. With flattery and hollow praise, the Judaizers were having some success with the Galatians, who we see in verse 16 make an enemy of Paul. If they could pull the Galatians completely away from Paul's influence, they could keep them under the Jewish law and coerce them to comply with circumcision. They could force the Galatians to become Jews in order to be called Christians. Without Paul in the picture, they could turn the Galatians into Judaizers themselves. The Judaizers were doing just what false teachers always do—making their own disciples.

Paul, however, wanted nothing for the Galatians except for them to hold to the gospel and become like Christ. Here is the difference between Paul and the Judaizers, both of whom had a profound influence over the Galatians: the Judaizers wanted the Galatians to become like them, and Paul wanted the Galatians to become like Christ. This is a good test for the people in our lives who influence us with their sermons, books, articles, and podcasts. Is their goal for us to conform to their particular brand of faith or to be conformed to the image of Christ? If they want us to subscribe to a list of rules and regulations to become the kind of Christian they claim to be, then their goal is like that of the Judaizers. They want us to become their disciples rather than disciples of Christ.

Paul's desire for the Galatians was different. It was not driven by pride or flattery. It was driven by the gospel. He wanted the Galatians to experience true freedom in Christ so that they could grow in maturity. He wanted Christ to be formed in them so that their lives would take the shape of Christ. He knew that their growth in Christ would change the way they lived and thought, and he longed for them to know that kind of freedom from both the law and their old, pagan ways of living. He did not just hope for that. He yearned for it as a mother in labor yearns for her child to be safely delivered. We have seen Paul make sharp rebukes and loving corrections, and now we see his tender, maternal appeal to the Galatians. He labored over them the first time when he visited and preached the gospel to them. But as they have begun turning away to a different gospel, he labors over them again. His concern for them is both pastoral and parental. Pastors who love their congregations will correct at any cost to keep their church members from falling into error.

Parents who love their children will do what is necessary to protect their children from danger. Paul's correction and investment in the Galatians were far beyond that of the Judaizers who only wanted to develop a larger following. Paul wants the Galatians to hold fast to Christ, to be changed by Christ, and to live through Christ so that they would one day see Christ face-to-face.

The process of being shaped by Christ takes time. That process, called sanctification, begins when we come to faith in Christ and continues until we see Him face-to-face. The word "sanctification" means "to be made holy," and as Christ is our standard of holiness and the one who has made us holy, to be sanctified means to become like Christ. God has given us what we need to be formed by Christ: the indwelling Holy Spirit in every believer, Scripture, access to God in prayer, and encouragement and exhortation from the church. The more we set our minds on Christ, learn about Christ, and love Christ, the more we will be formed by Him. Our lives will be shaped by Him rather than by the world around us. As Paul tells us in 1 Thessalonians 4:3, God's will for us is our sanctification—to be shaped by Christ. Paul's desire for the Galatians mirrored God's desire for the Galatians. And that should be our desire for ourselves and other believers as well.

AS WE GROW IN OUR KNOWLEDGE OF AND LOVE FOR HIM, OUR HEARTS ARE SHAPED BY CHRIST.

Read 1 Corinthians 2:10-16. How does being shaped by Christ change the way we think?

What is a good test for distinguishing between a false teacher and a true teacher of the gospel? What are some things to look out for if you are not sure whether someone is teaching the true gospel?

Sometimes we do not realize how much of our culture or society is influencing the way we think and live. Make a list of the primary people you listen to and the primary sources of information that you consume. List the messages each person or source gives. (For example: pastor, professor, friend, mentor, or a particular social media influencer, podcaster, or author.)

INFLUENCER	MESSAGE

CHRISTIANS ARE FREE AND
SHOULD LIVE FREELY

HAGAR AND SARAH

READ GALATIANS 4:21-27

If Paul has elevated any point in Galatians thus far, it is that Christians are free from the works of the law, sin, and pagan practices. Christians are free and should live freely. Paul has appealed to the Galatians to believe this through his testimony, logic, redemptive history, repeated gospel truths, and now, through the Judaizers' argument: the law. He fights fire with fire. He shows through the law that we do not need to hold to the law to be saved.

To understand what Paul is getting at in Galatians 4, we need to be familiar with the people and story he references from Genesis 16-17. We recall that Abraham was the man God promised to make the father of many nations and through whom all the people of the earth would be blessed (Genesis 12). We know that Jesus is the ultimate fulfillment and recipient of those promises and that He shared those promises with those who believe in Him for salvation. As Paul explains in Galatians 3:29, "if you belong to Christ, then you are Abraham's seed, heirs according to the promise." To the Jews, Abraham was their crowning glory. Their genetic relation to Abraham caused them to feel superior. Paul shows us in this passage, though, that it is not enough to be physical heirs of Abraham. Using the story of Abraham's sons from Genesis 16-17 and 21, Paul explains why continuing to live under the law enslaves, but living in Christ provides freedom.

From the account in Genesis, we learn that Abraham had two sons. Though God promised to give Abraham a son through whom He would fulfill His covenant, Abraham and Sarah were advanced in age and did not wait well for God to act. Sarah sent her handmaid, Hagar (an Egyptian slave), to sleep with her husband in order to conceive a child. Sarah figured she could raise the child as the one God promised since Abraham would be the father. Hagar conceived, but her son, Ishmael, was born a slave as she was and was not intended by God to be the child of the covenant. Years later, God gave Sarah the power to conceive and bear a son, Isaac, in her old age. Isaac was born free. Ishmael was born of the flesh, meaning that he was born of natural causes and intention. Isaac was born through promise, meaning that he was born through divine intention against the odds of natural causes since his mother had already passed the age of childbearing years.

Paul explains his allegory—Hagar and Sarah represent the old and new covenants, two Jerusalems, and slavery versus freedom. This passage in Galatians 4 is often called one of the most difficult to understand in the New Testament, but to put it succinctly, Hagar represents those who live under the old covenant and works of the law. They live in slavery and continue in slavery. These are the Jews who hold to the old covenant even though Christ had already come to fulfill it. Sarah represents those who are freed through the gospel of grace and have believed in Christ for the atonement of their sins. These are Christians who are part of the new, heavenly Jerusalem—the kingdom of God.

Everyone starts as an Ishmael, born into slavery to sin and the works of the law. But when God saves us and we believe in Jesus through faith, we are freed. There is no middle ground here. You are either an Ishmael or an Isaac. And some who believe they are an Isaac use the gospel as a means to curry favor with God. If we reduce Christianity to following rules and regulations to gain right standing with God, we are doing exactly as the Judaizers did. We are enslaving ourselves again when we have been freed. If we require others to follow our rules and regulations to be saved, we are becoming a type of Judaizer ourselves. The gospel has always been about freedom in Christ as we come to Him through faith alone.

Paul breaks into a chorus of praise at the end of this allegorical argument. While we might think at first glance that he is referring to Sarah, the barren woman, there is a deeper meaning to his quotation of Isaiah 54:1. While Sarah was a barren woman who became the mother of numerous children through the offspring of Isaac and his progeny, this verse refers to what God would do with the exiled Jews who were scattered across the land before the coming of Jesus. Isaiah's prophecy was partially fulfilled when the Jews regathered and rebuilt the wall in Jerusalem after the exile, but the ultimate fulfillment is ongoing now that Jesus has come. The children of Sarah continue to grow, for as Paul has already told us, those who belong to Christ are Abraham's offspring (Galatians 3:29). Abraham's offspring are those who have believed in Jesus for the forgiveness of sins. If you are a Christian, you are one of the children of the desolate woman!

Paul's verses of worship are appropriate in the middle of Galatians 4. When we see how the gospel of grace grafts us into the family of God, our hearts should respond with worship and praise. We are afforded the blessing of complete freedom when we believe in Jesus. Just as the barren woman, Sarah, received the miraculous gift of motherhood in Genesis 21, we receive the miraculous gift of salvation by faith in Jesus Christ, which makes us children of Abraham and children of God's covenantal promises. It only comes by grace through faith in Christ.

WHEN WE SEE HOW THE GOSPEL OF GRACE GRAFTS US INTO THE FAMILY OF GOD, OUR HEARTS SHOULD RESPOND WITH WORSHIP AND PRAISE.

What are some ways we reduce the Christian faith to a list of rules and regulations to follow? Why is this at odds with the gospel of grace?

_____

_____

_____

_____

_____

Read 2 Peter 1:3-11. How can we pursue godliness and spiritual growth without trying to turn the Christian life into a to-do list to gain God's favor?

_____

_____

_____

_____

_____

Write out your own prayer of spontaneous praise to God for including you in His family by grace through faith in Jesus. If you are not a believer, reflect on what it is that keeps you from believing in Jesus.

_____

_____

_____

_____

_____

FAITH IN CHRIST IS ENOUGH

CHILDREN OF PROMISE

Knowing who we are in Christ influences the way we live. Many of Paul's letters begin with explanations of the gospel, descriptions of who we are in Christ as opposed to who we used to be, and reminders of where our Christian identity is now rooted. Then, there is usually a shift in Paul's letters that moves to Christian living in light of Christian identity. We will see just such a shift in Galatians 5. Yet, before we get there, Paul gives the Galatians one more reminder of who we are in Jesus before explaining the implications of our new identity.

Paul addressed the Galatian Christians again, this time with affection, calling them "brothers and sisters." As believers in Jesus, they were siblings in Christ and related to Paul through faith. They are like Isaac—children of promise. And because they are children of promise, they are heirs with Christ and will receive all of the blessings promised to Abraham. Only through faith in Christ do we become children of promise. There is no other way, and this was always God's intent. "For every one of God's promises is 'Yes' in [Jesus]" (2 Corinthians 1:20). God's promises are realized, known, and received through faith in Jesus. Good works will never move anyone from the position of a slave to the status of a son. The Galatians came into the family of God through faith in Jesus, and that was the foundation of their status as children of promise.

What does that mean for the Galatians' present situation? Like Isaac, they should have expected persecution. But they could endure persecution because they had an eternal inheritance. Continuing his allegory from the story of Sarah, Hagar, and their sons, Paul notes that Isaac was persecuted by Ishmael. In Genesis 21, Ishmael, who was a young teen at the time, mocked his younger brother, Isaac, at a family feast. As a result, Sarah commanded that Hagar and Ishmael be driven out of the family, and they were. Paul says in Galatians 4 that as Ishmael persecuted Isaac, similar persecution was happening now. The children of the flesh were persecuting the children of promise. This is precisely what the Judaizers were doing to the Galatians; they were persecuting them by seeking to enslave them to the works of the law in order to be saved. What is the right response to those who seek to enslave others to religion and rituals? Paul tells us the Scriptural response is to drive them out. He quotes from Genesis 21 saying, "Drive out this slave with her son, for the son of this slave will not be a coheir with the son of a free woman."

Is Paul being too harsh? When it came to his concern for the Galatians, not at all. The Judaizers were pulling the Galatians toward false religion. This was a primary gospel issue and one worth taking a hard stance upon because the souls of the Galatians were at stake. Paul did not want them to be lulled into believing that they could earn their favor with God. Right standing before God only comes through faith in Christ. When it comes to false teaching today, we must be just as firm as Paul. For Christians to live freely in Christ, we can make no room for those who infiltrate the church and seek to enslave believers with the bonds of legalism. Works righteousness is a false gospel and will always be a dead-end for those who yoke themselves to it. Paul says that those who are enslaved to the law will never be heirs with Christ. Only children of promise—those who are awakened to faith in Christ as a result of the Spirit's work in their hearts—will inherit God's promises.

Paul closes chapter 4 by addressing his brothers and sisters in Christ again, for this is who he believes them to be—children of promise. They are free in Christ and must not succumb to the false teaching of the Judaizers. They do not need the false teaching of the Judaizers. They have everything they need in Jesus. The same is true for us. All that is required for us to have right standing before God is faith in Jesus. All that is required for us to be declared righteous is faith in Jesus. All that is required for us to be moved from slave to son is faith in Jesus. Anyone who teaches that we must do more to be justified is teaching a false gospel. If we are teaching or believing that someone must do more than believe in Jesus to be saved, then we are in error.

When we get to a passage like Galatians 4 that compares and contrasts those who hold to truth and those who do not, it is good for us to take spiritual stock and ask ourselves some hard questions. Though we all begin like Ishmael—slaves to sin and works of the law—the Lord can move us to become an Isaac—a child of promise who lives freely in Christ. Are you an Ishmael, or are you an Isaac? Are you an Isaac who lives like an Ishmael? Have you enslaved yourself to religious practices that will never bring you more favor with God?

Paul's closing words to the Galatians should resonate with us, too. If we have believed in Jesus for the atonement of our sins, we need to do nothing else to be made righteous before God. Faith in Christ is enough, and as a result of such faith, we are free children of promise. Our lives will look differently as a result of that faith but not until we have been changed by that faith. We do not change ourselves and work really hard to come to Christ. No, we come to Christ to be changed.

KNOWING WHO WE ARE IN CHRIST INFLUENCES THE WAY WE LIVE.

Give some examples of false teaching that you have seen infiltrate the church today.
Why is it dangerous to entertain that kind of teaching?

Read Romans 8:16-17. What do these verses say about who believers are in Christ?

Are you an Isaac or an Ishmael? Or, are you an Isaac who lives like an Ishmael?
Explain your answer below.

NOW YOU TOO,
BROTHERS AND SISTERS,
LIKE ISAAC, ARE
CHILDREN OF PROMISE.

—

GALATIANS 4:28

WEEKLY REFLECTION

REVIEW GALATIANS 4:8-31

Paraphrase the passage from this week.

What did you observe from this week's text about God and His character?

What does this week's passage reveal about the condition of mankind and yourself?

How does this passage point to the gospel?

How should you respond to this passage? What specific action steps can you take this week to apply this passage?

Write a prayer in response to your study of God's Word. Adore God for who He is, confess sins that He has revealed in your own life, ask Him to empower you to walk in obedience, and pray for anyone who came to mind as you studied.

THIS IS REAL FREEDOM

FREED TO BE FREE

READ GALATIANS 5:1-6

One day, all human beings will stand before God to receive His final judgment over their lives (Revelation 17:8, 20:11-15). There is only one thing that will matter on that day: how will you be justified before God, the holy and sovereign judge? We have learned that there is only one way to be justified, and that is by faith alone in Christ alone. It will not matter how tenaciously you held to your views on baptism or church government or what kind of music you thought was appropriate for worship. On that day, it will not matter how many theological books you read or how often you tithed. It will not matter if you preferred this political party or that view of creation. While all of those issues are important in their proper place, they do not hold the primary position of justification by faith. What will matter on the day of God's judgment is whether or not you believed that Jesus's sacrifice alone was enough to pay for your sins. Or, as Paul put it, "faith working through love" (Galatians 5:6).

Of all the things on which we ought to dig in our heels, justification by faith alone in Christ alone should top the list. Our freedom in Christ from guilt, sin, and works of the law hinges upon our belief in Jesus's sacrifice at the cross. We can only be free if Jesus sets us free (John 8:34-36). As Paul has labored to communicate in Galatians 1-4, there is no other way to be declared righteous before God. We cannot make ourselves righteous. We can only believe with faith that Jesus's death in our place paid our debt for our sin. Circumcision will not do it. Obeying the law will not do it. Nor will any other good practice we adopt to find favor in God's eyes. Justification has only ever been accomplished by faith in Jesus. If we want to live as the free people God desires us to be, we must hold fast and stand firm on this foundational truth — that we are justified by faith alone in Christ alone.

Paul makes it clear in verse 2 that if we seek to add to what Jesus has done to make us righteous, then the sacrifice of Jesus is of no use to us. Pairing the cross with our good works devalues what Jesus died to accomplish. It invalidates grace. The Judaizers who were turning the Galatians away from the gospel of grace subscribed to the view that real Christians had to be circumcised (Acts 15:1,5). To that view, Paul says that they might as well keep the law too. His point is that trying to justify ourselves by any means other than faith in Christ severs us from the doctrine of grace. The very point of grace is that it is free and unearned. We cannot add to it without nullifying it. If Christians want to live free from guilt and sin, then they must reject the notion that they can do anything to earn that freedom. They can only believe in Jesus for freedom. That is the very reason He set us free—for freedom! To try to add to His work at the cross is to reject grace and Christ Himself. Salvation will always come through faith in Jesus plus nothing.

Where does our faith alone in Christ alone come from? Saving faith comes through the Holy Spirit (Galatians 5:5, Ephesians 2:8-9). We can, therefore, look to the day of God's judgment with great hope and anticipation because we have already been declared righteous and will fully stand in that righteousness before Him because of what Jesus has done for us on the cross. Christians do not have to fear death or judgment because our hope is in Christ's finished work on the cross, not our attempts at earning God's favor. Our sins have been forgiven, and we have been declared righteous by our God-given faith in Christ Jesus. Because of the faith provided by the Holy Spirit, we get to live in complete freedom.

Christian freedom, as we will see later in chapter 5, is not a license to live however we want. It is quite the opposite. Christian freedom reflects a life that has been changed by faith in Christ and will be evidenced by love and good works. Again, it is important to note that Paul is not advocating for love as a requirement for justification. He is not adding love to the requirements for salvation any more than he is adding either circumcision or uncircumcision. Nothing can be added to justification by faith. We cannot hold any position or secondary belief as equal to justification by faith. We are saved by faith alone, and true, saving faith will always be evidenced by love and good deeds. Our Christian freedom from sin and guilt will not give us a license to live selfishly or sinfully. Rather, true freedom in Christ will change our affections and tastes. It will aid us in putting our sin to death and loving Christ and others more than we love ourselves. It will result in care for others, in selfless living, in the worship of God rather than self or selfish desires. We will begin to live by faith just as we were justified by faith—by the power of the Holy Spirit. This is real freedom.

OF ALL THE THINGS ON WHICH WE OUGHT TO DIG IN OUR HEELS, JUSTIFICATION BY FAITH ALONE IN CHRIST ALONE SHOULD TOP THE LIST.

Read Romans 8:1-4. Why could the law not free us from sin and death?
What did God do to set us free?

Read Revelation 17:8 and 20:11-15. Do you fear God's final judgment over your life?
Why or why not?

Why is it important to stand firm on the truth that Christ has freed us from slavery to sin and the works of the law? How does legalism in the church undermine that truth?

WE MUST BECOME STUDENTS
OF THE BIBLE

FINISH WELL

READ GALATIANS 5:7-12

In Scripture, the Christian life is often compared to running a race. The goal in any race is to finish well, even when faced with obstacles like fatigue, distractions, or injury. For a long-distance race like a marathon or an ultra of 50 or 100 miles, runners must train well, pace themselves, avoid anything that weighs or slows them down, and keep their eyes on the finish line. Even if you are not a runner, you can probably see the parallels in the Christian life. We experience many distractions, obstacles, and sufferings that can potentially block our perseverance toward the finish line. But the call for every believer is to finish well the race that God has set before us.

This exhortation to finish well comes as a warning from Paul in chapter 5. Blocked and distracted by the false teaching of the Judaizers, the Galatians were straying from the gospel path. According to Paul, they had been running well, but the false teachers were persuading them to step off the course that would lead them to the finish line of faithfulness. His goal in writing was to help them stay the course and hold fast to faith in Christ without stumbling over any false teaching that would prevent them from finishing well. He warns them that the persuasion to believe in any route to justification besides faith in Christ alone is a dead-end, not from God. Remember back in chapter 1, that it is God who calls the Galatians to a saving faith in Jesus Christ (Galatians 1:6). Any call to believe in salvation through a different means cannot be of God.

False teaching is not something to treat flippantly, nor is it something to ignore. Paul likens the pervasiveness of false teaching to leaven in a lump of bread dough. It only takes a small amount of leavening agent like yeast to permeate an entire lump of dough. The whole loaf will rise because of that tiny amount of yeast. Similarly, a small amount of false teaching can infiltrate and infect an entire church, leading many astray if it is not dealt with immediately. False teaching, whatever it might look like in a church setting, is dangerous because it can cause a believer who professes faith in Christ and is running the race well to become confused, distracted, and eventually detoured from the finish line. Paul is not saying that the Galatians are in danger of losing their salvation. Saving faith is a gift of God that cannot be undermined by man. However, when a professing believer embraces false teaching that does not align with Scriptural truth, it might reveal that the person was not a true believer in the first place. Yet Paul is confident that this does not describe the Galatians. He believes they would continue in the true faith (Galatians 5:10). That is not to say that the false teachers were not still dangerous. In fact, Paul is confident that the Judaizers who were trying to convince the Galatians to submit to circumcision and works as a means of justification will be judged by God for their error.

We have seen Paul's concern for the Galatians escalate at times throughout his letter, and in verse 12, he is about as harsh as we can imagine. While his words seem crude, his exasperation with false teaching communicates both his love for the Galatians and his commitment to the pure, unadulterated gospel of Christ. If the Judaizers were requiring rituals like circumcision for salvation, then he hoped the knife might slip a little and harm them for the harm they are inflicting on the eternal state of the Galatians. He was using an analogy here—not threatening physical violence. Under Old Testament law, eunuchs were not allowed into the temple (Deuteronomy 23:1). It may have been that Paul was using hyperbole to say that those who require circumcision should not be allowed in the church. Whatever his intent in using such a harsh remark, the point is crystal clear. False teaching is dangerous and has no place in the church. It must be dealt with aggressively before it infects the entire body of Christ and leads many astray.

Surprisingly, a rumor was floating around the Galatian church that Paul himself preached circumcision. The Judaizers likely circulated this rumor to garner the Galatians' trust in their false message. But Paul was being persecuted widely for preaching the gospel only; he would never add circumcision to the gospel message. He knew the gospel was offensive, and if he softened its message by preaching works or requirements beyond faith for justification, he would not be suffering for such a message. Paul was committed to the gospel in its true form—salvation by faith alone in Christ alone. With his eyes set on the finish line of faith, he had nothing to lose that mattered to him. He wished the same for the Galatians: to finish the race of faith well, free from the entanglements of sin or false beliefs.

Like the author of Hebrews encourages us to "lay aside every hindrance and the sin that so easily ensnares us," Paul hoped the Galatians would remove the hindrance of false teachers from their presence and hold fast to the gospel of Jesus (Hebrews 12:1). When it comes to living the Christian life, we will face many such entanglements. The only way to press forward in perseverance is to keep "our eyes on Jesus, the source and perfecter of our faith" (Hebrews 12:2). If we are not sure whether what we are hearing from the pulpit, reading in a book or article, or listening to on a podcast is biblically sound, we must look to the source—Jesus—to learn to practice discernment. We must become students of the Bible, confident in the truth of the gospel so that we can lay aside the snare of false teaching and finish the race well.

THE CALL FOR EVERY BELIEVER IS TO FINISH WELL THE RACE THAT GOD HAS SET BEFORE US.

Read Hebrews 12:1-2. How do we finish the race of faith well when faced with sin and distractions?

How do we keep our eyes on Jesus and the gospel? List some ways.

False teaching in your current context might look different than what the Galatians faced. Sometimes false teaching can look like taking a neutral or secondary issue and promoting it to a primary place of conviction. What are some errors or misplaced convictions that have pervaded your circles of influence? (Some examples might include legalism, ancestor or saint worship, modes or methods of baptism, music choices, educational convictions, etc.)

RUNNING THE RACE

When we come to faith in Jesus Christ, we begin running the race of the Christian life. As we follow Jesus, we become more and more like Him. This process of growth in our life is called sanctification. God uses many things in our lives to conform us into the image of His Son, and we learn to endure many kinds of trials as we walk closely with Him. However, we will also encounter obstacles to our perseverance, and we must heed Scripture's call to keep running with endurance. To lay aside sin, apathy, and the allure of false teaching, we must stay on the course of the true gospel, keeping our eyes fixed on Jesus. To endure suffering and sorrows along the way, we will find help from the Holy Spirit, comfort from Scripture, and encouragement from fellow saints. The Lord has equipped us with everything we need to run the race of faith and finish well!

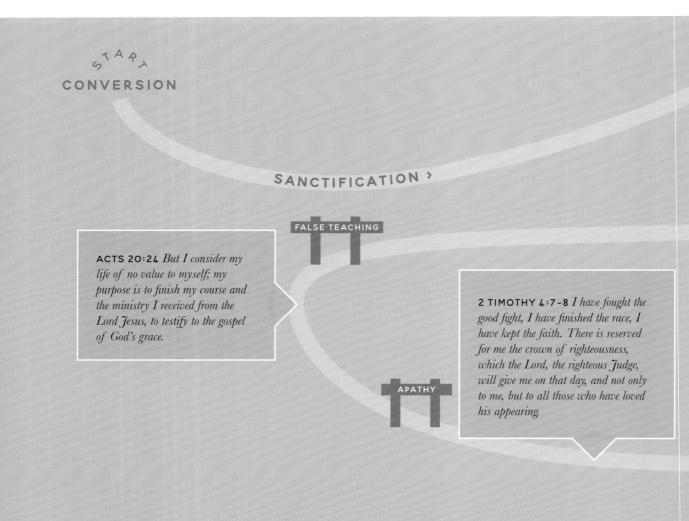

START

CONVERSION

SANCTIFICATION ›

FALSE TEACHING

ACTS 20:24 *But I consider my life of no value to myself; my purpose is to finish my course and the ministry I received from the Lord Jesus, to testify to the gospel of God's grace.*

2 TIMOTHY 4:7-8 *I have fought the good fight, I have finished the race, I have kept the faith. There is reserved for me the crown of righteousness, which the Lord, the righteous Judge, will give me on that day, and not only to me, but to all those who have loved his appearing.*

APATHY

I CORINTHIANS 9:24-27 *Don't you know that the runners in a stadium all race, but only one receives the prize? Run in such a way to win the prize. Now everyone who competes exercises self-control in everything. They do it to receive a perishable crown, but we an imperishable crown. So I do not run like one who runs aimlessly or box like one beating the air. Instead, I discipline my body and bring it under strict control, so that after preaching to others, I myself will not be disqualified.*

SUFFERING

SIN

HEBREWS 12:1-2 *Therefore, since we also have such a large cloud of witnesses surrounding us, let us lay aside every hindrance and the sin that so easily ensnares us. Let us run with endurance the race that lies before us, keeping our eyes on Jesus, the source and perfecter of our faith. For the joy that lay before him, he endured the cross, despising the shame, and sat down at the right hand of the throne of God.*

DISCOURAGEMENT

JAMES 1:12 *Blessed is the one who endures trials, because when he has stood the test he will receive the crown of life that God has promised to those who love him.*

GLORIFICATION

FINISH

WE BELONG TO GOD WHO
LOVES US

FREE TO LOVE

READ GALATIANS 5:13-15

Freedom is not really freedom if it is used in the wrong way. We can actually abuse freedom in such a way that enslaves us once again. The freedom we have received in Christ relieves us from trying to justify ourselves through works of the law. That freedom does not give us the liberty to live however we want. Jesus said, "everyone who commits sin is a slave of sin" (John 8:34). Christian freedom does not enslave us to that from which Christ died to free us. True Christian freedom does not lead to sinful living. This was what the Galatians needed to hear, and it is what we need to hear as well.

Paul's shift from identity to calling occurs in Galatians 5:13. Though he has spent four chapters warning against legalism, he moves to commands for Christian living that would protect the Galatians from the polar opposite of legalism: licentiousness. If legalism is life without access to freedom, then licentiousness is life without limits of freedom at all. Legalism enslaves to works, and licentiousness enslaves to sinful living. Slipping to either side of true Christian freedom is a danger to our souls. Paul appeals to the Galatians to use the freedom they have received in Christ as an opportunity to obey God by loving others.

We might think that we can now live however we want because we have already been justified by faith. Does it matter how we live since we are free from trying to make ourselves right before God? Can we not just live and let live? Can we explore the delights of sinful pleasure and treat others with disregard since trying to obey the law will not make us right before God? It might be tempting to think that way, but we were not saved by grace through faith to indulge in sin for which Christ died. To use liberty as an occasion to sin is to live in direct opposition to the freedom Jesus bought for us with His blood. He freed us to stop trying to justify ourselves through works. He made us children of God and co-heirs with Him of all the promises God made to Abraham. As children of God, we are free from sin and works of the law, but we do not belong to ourselves. We belong to God who loves us. And our response to His love should be love as well.

How do we love as a response to the freedom we have received through the gospel of Jesus? We obey Him. Jesus said in John 14:15, "If you love me, you will keep my commands." To avoid legalism, we must remember that we do not love in an attempt to gain God's favor. Rather, we love because in Christ we already have God's favor. Obedience to God's commands is a right response to God's favor and evidence of our love for Him. Because the Holy Spirit lives in every believer, we are enabled and equipped to love Christ by obeying His commands. As Paul tells us in Galatians 5:13, we have been freed in order to love and serve others. This is how we obey God's law.

Now, you might be thinking that it seemed Paul told us not to enslave ourselves to the law. Indeed, the law could not justify us before God. We are justified by faith in Christ. However, that does not mean we should disobey God's law. In its proper place, the law can lead us to obedience once we have already been justified by faith in Jesus. Obedience to the law can be a means of our sanctification—that process of being made like Jesus. In this way, we are not under the law but fulfilling it. What better way to obey God in love than to love our brothers and sisters in Christ? Paul brings part of the law found in Leviticus 19:18 into Galatians 5:14, stating that "the whole law is fulfilled in one statement: Love your neighbor as yourself." We obey God by loving others. Though we cannot be justified by the law, we are still commanded by God to love. His commands are always for our good. Rather than using our freedom as an opportunity to live however we want without any regard for others, we are free to care for our siblings in Christ as the fruit of the new life we have received in Jesus.

Biblical love does not always look like contemporary definitions of love. First, Christian love is a response to God's love (1 John 4:11). Second, it is displayed in how we treat others better than ourselves. 1 Corinthians 13 tells us that Christian love is patient and kind. It is humble and selfless. It keeps no record of wrongs nor does it rejoice in the calamities of others. It is not irritable or envious. Biblical love requires sacrifice. Jesus modeled this kind of love for us. He told His disciples, "Love one another as I have loved you. No one has greater love than this: to lay down his life for his friends" (John 15:12-13). This selfless, encouraging, sacrificial, patient, forgiving, enduring love is how we express the freedom we have in Christ. Because the Spirit lives in us, we can exercise this kind of love in response to God's great love for us. This is true freedom in Christ.

Legalism keeps us under the reign of fruitless works. Licentiousness rules our hearts with selfish, depraved living. In Christ, however, we are free from trying to gain God's approval and free to love others with sacrificial love as we have been loved. As followers of Christ, we will be known by our love for one another because it will reflect to the watching world the image of our Savior who loves us and gave Himself for us.

WE WERE NOT SAVED BY GRACE THROUGH FAITH TO INDULGE IN SIN FOR WHICH CHRIST DIED.

Define legalism in your own words. Define licentiousness in your own words. Why are both of these ways of living both dangerous for our souls and at odds with the gospel of Jesus?

Read Romans 8:3-4. How is the law "fulfilled in us" if we have been justified by faith? How can we walk in obedience to God without erring on the side of legalism?

List some ways you can sacrificially love your brothers and sisters in Christ. Be specific, and try to follow through on a few of those ways this week.

WALK WITH HIM

WALK BY THE SPIRIT

READ GALATIANS 5:16-18

Do you ever feel that you know what the right thing to do is, yet somewhere inside you lurks a desire to do the wrong thing even though you know it is wrong? Before we come to faith in Christ, we are not concerned about our sinfulness. We serve ourselves and cater to our passions. Even our good actions are tainted by sinful motives and desires. However, once we come to faith in Christ, we are suddenly at war with who we used to be. Though we have been freed from sin and the curse of the law, we still fight against our sinful desires each and every day.

Sometimes, Christians can feel defeated in their war against sin. We might even wonder if true victory is possible. Paul gives us the promise we need to continue in the war against our sinful desires: "walk by the Spirit and you will certainly not carry out the desire of the flesh" (Galatians 5:16). The Greek word for "walk" in this verse is *peripateō*, which literally means "to walk around." To walk by the Spirit means to walk with Him. Or, as Paul will put it later in verse 18, to be "led by" Him.

Who is the Spirit? The Holy Spirit is the third member of the Godhead, or the Trinity. He is not the Father; neither is He the Son. He is the Spirit of God and is fully divine. He inspired men to write the Scriptures without error. He calls people to faith in Christ and makes them alive in Christ through faith. Jesus promised that the Holy Spirit would come after He returned to heaven, and since Pentecost in Acts 2, every believer is given the gift of the Spirit at conversion. He dwells in us, giving comfort and helping us to understand the Bible and obey Christ faithfully until we go to be with God in heaven forever. The Holy Spirit is the teacher, guide, and helper of every person who has placed faith in Jesus for the forgiveness of sins. He enables us to put our sin to death. We have been given an indescribable gift in the constant presence of the Holy Spirit in our lives!

Paul promises us that if we are walking by the Spirit, we will certainly not carry out the desires of our flesh. The flesh refers to who we were before we were justified by faith—our natural, sinful selves who lived for selfish desires at odds with God's holiness. Those desires we had before coming to faith in Christ will rear their ugly heads, but because Jesus had victory over sin, Satan, and death on the cross, we do not have to give ourselves to those desires the way we once did when we were enslaved to them. And because the Spirit dwells in us, we can now say no to those desires we used to satisfy ourselves outside of God's sufficiency. As we say no to those desires, we have confidence—not in ourselves or our attempts at obedience—but in the power of the Holy Spirit who will help us overcome. The confidence written into Paul's promise in verse 16 is rooted in the power of the Spirit, not us. If we are walking closely with Him, being led by Him, and fighting sin with His strength, then we will certainly not give ourselves to sinful passions and desires.

Paul tells us what some of those desires and passions are later in chapter 5, but the important thing to note in verse 17 is that Christians should expect to be at war with their sin. Every Christian should expect a regular, ongoing fight with sin. Remember, Paul is talking to the Galatian Christians here. Their flesh desired what was opposed to the Holy Spirit just as we have desires in opposition to the Spirit. We struggle to obey God because our flesh desires disobedience. But this is why confidence in the Spirit's power is so encouraging. We are not at war by ourselves. We do not have to depend on our own power to overcome our sinful desires. If the Spirit dwells in us, then we have been freed from the curse of sin under the law. On the days we feel discouraged in our fight against sin, we can remember that fighting sin is a normal part of the Christian life. We have been changed and made new, and our lives will reflect the ongoing transformation as the Spirit works in us.

How do we walk by the Spirit? We remind ourselves over and over of the freedom and grace that come from the promises of God. Meditating on God's promises keeps the truth of the gospel ever before us. Setting Scripture before our hearts and minds regularly reminds us of what is true about God and ourselves. We get so many mixed messages from the world around us. We are easily distracted by what our culture has to offer, and the allure of fulfilling our selfish desires can dilute our affections for Christ. We must wage war against those temptations by turning our faces to the powerful and faithful promises of God so that we may stand firm upon the gospel.

When it comes to that daily fight against sin, know that you are not alone. You have been freed from sin, equipped with the truth of Scripture, and are being led by the victorious Holy Spirit. One day, we will be completely free from our struggle with sin, but until that day, we can walk in confidence with the Holy Spirit.

BECAUSE THE SPIRIT DWELLS IN US, WE CAN NOW SAY NO TO THOSE DESIRES WE USED TO SATISFY OURSELVES OUTSIDE OF GOD'S SUFFICIENCY.

Why are the flesh and the Spirit at odds with one another? Why should Christians expect this kind of inner struggle?

Read Romans 7:14-25. If Paul is referring to himself as a believer here, what can we learn about the war we must fight with sin? Why must we fight?

How do we walk by the Spirit?

WE CANNOT PRODUCE FRUIT
WITHOUT ABIDING IN HIM

THE WORKS OF THE FLESH AND THE FRUIT OF THE SPIRIT

READ GALATIANS 5:19-25

You can identify a tree by the kind of fruit it produces. If a tree has apples hanging from its branches, it is safe to assume it is an apple tree. Jesus used this kind of analogy in His Sermon on the Mount, identifying false prophets by the bad fruit they produced (Matthew 7:15-20). Diseased trees bear bad fruit, and healthy trees bear good fruit. Our lives will produce evidence in keeping with our hearts. If we are walking in the Spirit, we will bear the Spirit's fruit. If we are running after sin, our lives will produce the bad fruit of sinful works.

Paul tells us in Galatians 5 that it will be obvious if we are keeping in step with the Spirit or not. In verses 19-21, he gives us a list of sinful vices that are obvious works of the flesh. Remember, the term "flesh" here refers to our sinful nature. While Paul's list is not exhaustive (which we can tell by the way he tagged "and anything similar" to the end of the list), the fifteen works of the flesh fall into four categories that pertain to sexual sins, devotional sins of worship, relational sins, and sins of overindulgence.

Paul is clear in verse 21 that anyone who practices these sinful behaviors and heart attitudes will not inherit the kingdom of God. It is one thing to wrestle with a besetting sin, to keep fighting it though you have failures now and then. It is another thing altogether to give yourself to that sin. That is what Paul means by "practice." If you build your life around a regular practice of sin without remorse, repentance, or any attempt at fighting it, you will not inherit the kingdom of God. Habitually seeking to satisfy the desires of the flesh through sexual immorality, envy, hatred, idolatry, or drunkenness reveal a heart enslaved to sin. The flesh and the Spirit are at odds, remember? We cannot give ourselves to sin and claim to be walking with the Spirit. If we are in Christ, we have been made new. We will seek, through the power of the Spirit, to reject and renounce our former ways of living. Rather than running toward our sin, we will run toward Christ.

This list was not news to the Galatians. Paul had already warned them about practicing sinful lifestyles when he visited them the first time. Freedom in Christ was never meant to lead one to licentious living. True followers of Jesus will still struggle with sin, as we saw in yesterday's passage, but a new life in Christ will result in regular repentance and a desire to put one's sin to death. Rather than giving oneself to sin, true believers in Jesus will produce a different kind of fruit—the fruit that comes from the Holy Spirit Himself. In verses 22-23, Paul lists nine virtues that will grow and mature in the life of a believer who walks in the Spirit. These virtues can be grouped in triads pertaining to God, others, and self. Love, joy, and peace grow from one's contentment in God alone. Patience, kindness, and goodness bloom in a believer's treatment of others. Faithfulness, gentleness, and self-control are cultivated in the heart of a believer who lives with restraint and steadfastness.

The fruit of the Spirit is not something for us to examine and work on. For instance, we are not to gauge how we are doing on each virtue and then buckle down to work harder on something like patience or kindness. Notice that the fruit belongs to the Spirit. The fruit grows from Him and through Him. As we spend time with the Lord in study, prayer, meditation on the Word, and in fellowship with other believers, we will become like the One from whom the fruit is derived. The more we get to know Him and spend time with Him, the more like Him we become. Jesus said in John 15:1-5 that we cannot produce fruit without abiding in Him. We abide through the regular intake and deep study of Scripture, through prayer and intercession, through meditation on the Word, and through fellowship with other believers. As we abide in Him, we know Him more deeply and are changed by Him. In that way, His fruit begins to grow and mature in our lives. We can only do this through the Spirit's power and strength.

That does not mean that we live passively. Our Christian life involves being led by and actively following Christ. Those who belong to Christ are called to crucify the passions of the flesh. This call to crucify our flesh calls to mind the grisly act of crucifixion. Death by crucifixion is long and slow. But it is also final. While our sinful natures were nailed to the cross of Christ (Galatians 2:20), we will fight temptations to go back and attempt to breathe life back into those dying selves. Our call in Galatians 5 is to remember that we belong to Christ and that we must leave the corpses of our sinful desires on the cross. We must forsake them by turning fully to Christ each day. God has given us the means of abiding in Christ so that the fruit of the Spirit grows in our lives rather than the works of the flesh. Through the power of the Spirit, we can follow where He leads as He cultivates the evidence of true, saving faith in our hearts. By His grace, we will bear His fruit as we keep in step with Him each day.

OUR LIVES WILL PRODUCE EVIDENCE IN KEEPING WITH OUR HEARTS.

Read John 15:1-5. How do we bear fruit? Is it completely up to us? What is our involvement in the growth of fruit in our lives?

What steps have you taken to forsake sin in your life? How are you fighting it daily?

In the chart on the next page, list the works of the flesh and the fruit of the Spirit in their corresponding columns. What, if anything, do you notice about the lists? List some ways the works of the flesh and fruit of the Spirit are at odds with each other.

WORKS OF THE FLESH (verses 19-21)	FRUIT OF THE SPIRIT (verses 22-23)

List any observations or differences you find in the two lists.

IF WE
LIVE BY
THE SPIRIT,
LET US
ALSO KEEP
IN STEP
WITH
THE SPIRIT

I SAY THEN, WALK BY
THE SPIRIT AND YOU
WILL CERTAINLY NOT
CARRY OUT THE DESIRE
OF THE FLESH.

—

GALATIANS 5:16

WEEKLY REFLECTION

REVIEW GALATIANS 5:1-25

Paraphrase the passage from this week.

What did you observe from this week's text about God and His character?

What does this week's passage reveal about the condition of mankind and yourself?

How does this passage point to the gospel?

How should you respond to this passage? What specific action steps can you take this week to apply this passage?

Write a prayer in response to your study of God's Word. Adore God for who He is, confess sins that He has revealed in your own life, ask Him to empower you to walk in obedience, and pray for anyone who came to mind as you studied.

CONSIDER OTHERS

BURDEN-BEARING

READ GALATIANS 5:26-6:5

In Galatians 5-6, we find a direct correlation between walking in the Spirit and loving the body of Christ. Paul moves from what it means to walk in the Spirit to the effect that walking in the Spirit has on our relationships within the church. In his address of "brothers and sisters," Paul reminds us that we are the family of God, and as we abide in Christ and walk in the Spirit, the fruit that grows in our lives is for the benefit of our siblings in Christ.

Paul begins by teaching how brothers and sisters in Christ are not to behave toward one another. Specifically, we are to avoid all forms of conceit—of thinking more highly of ourselves than we should. Conceit has a detrimental effect on our relationships with other believers, especially in regard to provoking one another and envying one another. We can be conceited in thinking we are better, smarter, more spiritual, or more valuable than others, leading us to feel superior to others. We can also envy others for their status, maturity, or gifts, leading us to become resentful in our relationships. Either way, a misguided view of ourselves can be poisonous to our Christian relationships.

Paul says that if we think we are something when we are nothing, we are deceiving ourselves. He says in other epistles that we should not think of ourselves too highly but ought to consider others better than ourselves (Romans 12:3, Philippians 2:3). Perhaps it sounds harsh to hear that we are nothing, but without the Spirit opening our eyes to see our sinful state before a holy God, we truly are nothing and can do nothing about our sin. We are desperately dependent upon God, who made a way for us to know Him and be reconciled to Him through faith in Jesus. Paul is not being harsh. He is being truthful about our condition before Christ and eliminating any reason we think we might have to treat others in an inferior manner. These biblical commands help us to see ourselves and our brothers and sisters correctly before God, giving us the right frame of mind for love and sacrifice in serving others.

Rather than being puffed up with conceit that leads to envy and provocation, Paul shows us how walking in the Spirit should inform our behavior toward one another. In verse 2, He commands us to "carry one another's burdens." This command comes on the heels of a specific way of obeying the command through the act of restoration. Verse 2 implies that we will all have burdens that we need help carrying. We were not meant to carry them alone. Jesus carried our ultimate burden to the cross, paying for our sins and freeing us from the curse of sin under the law. But Jesus also promised that we would have suffering in this world (John 16:33), and we need help from the family of God to walk through that suffering. When we view our brothers and sisters in Christ with love rather than conceit, we will seek out ways to help them carry their burdens. Paul says that in so doing, we "will fulfill the law of Christ." Now Paul is not talking about being saved by keeping the Old Testament law. He calls us back to the very words of Jesus who commanded us to love one another. Jesus said, "I give you a new command: Love one another. Just as I have loved you, you are also to love one another" (John 13:34). In Galatians 5:14, Paul summed up the whole law in a command to love our neighbors as ourselves. We do not obey the commands of Scripture to be saved but because we have been saved. Those who walk in the Spirit will gladly and sacrificially love others by carrying their burdens. Rather than indulging in the sinful works of the flesh, those who walk in the Spirit bear the Spirit's fruit for the benefit of those around them. They exercise the Spirit-grown fruit of love and kindness toward those who are suffering by seeking to bear their burdens.

Paul gives a more specific example of this Spirit-led burden-bearing in Galatians 6:1. He exhorts those who are spiritual to exercise gentleness in restoring the person who has been overtaken by sin. "You who are spiritual" can refer to those who are more mature in Christ, but truthfully, anyone who belongs to Christ has the Spirit dwelling in them. Thus, every Christian is spiritual. Those who are being led by the Spirit and are actively following Him can carefully and gently restore someone who has been caught up in sin, being wary of falling into sin themselves. This kind of restoration requires care, investments of time and prayer, humility, and awareness of one's own temptations to sin. But as we see in Matthew 18:15-20 and James 5:19-20, restoration is a worthy process and demonstrates deep love and care for the one who has wandered into sin.

We can bear the burdens of other believers in many ways. But that means that we must be actively involved in the lives of our church family. We must fight the temptation to think we are too busy or self-important to practice burden-bearing. Rather, we must walk in the Spirit, seeking ways to care for others who are suffering and reaching out to those who are wandering in sin. In doing so, the fruit of the Spirit is demonstrated in our lives in love for the family of God.

THOSE WHO WALK IN THE SPIRIT WILL GLADLY AND SACRIFICIALLY LOVE OTHERS BY CARRYING THEIR BURDENS.

Read James 2:1-13. How does the sin of favoritism keep us from bearing the burdens of others?

How can you practically bear the burdens of your local church family? List some specific ways you can carry the burdens of others this week.

Do you have trouble sharing your own burdens with others? How does our transparency help other believers to obey Paul's command in Galatians 6:2?

TRUE SAVING FAITH WILL RESULT IN
GOOD WORKS AND SPIRIT-LED LIVING

SOWING AND REAPING

READ GALATIANS 6:6-10

Sowing and reaping is a law of nature set forth by God. We will always reap the fruits of the type of seeds we sow. We will never plant corn in the spring and reap tomatoes in the fall. Neither can we expect a harvest if we never plant anything. That is not how it works in the physical world, and that is not how it works in our spiritual lives either. We cannot cultivate sinful behavior in our daily living and expect to see a harvest of good spiritual fruit.

Paul uses the analogy of sowing and reaping to help us further understand what it looks like to walk in the Spirit rather than the flesh. Sowing to the flesh brings about destruction while sowing to the Spirit will bring about a harvest of eternal life from the Spirit. What does it mean to sow to the flesh? Remember the command to crucify the flesh and its passions in Galatians 5:24? Our sins are nailed to the cross, dying a slow death as we walk in the Spirit and obey the commands of Scripture. Sowing to the flesh means returning to those sinful desires and breathing life back into them. As we coddle and give mental space to those desires, we allow them to dominate our life.

Consider James's words: "But each person is tempted when he is drawn away and enticed by his own evil desire. Then after desire has conceived, it gives birth to sin, and when sin is fully grown, it gives birth to death" (James 1:14-15). Sinful desires lead to sinful actions that lead to spiritual death. If we are sowing seeds of sinful desires, we will reap a harvest of destruction. It begins with what we allow to occupy our minds. If we entertain lustful thoughts or hold grudges in anger, we are sowing to the flesh. If we fantasize about a person or situation that we covet, we are sowing to the flesh. If we are consumed with our appearance or what others think about us, we are sowing to the flesh. If we only think about work and financial gain, we are sowing to the flesh. If we constantly indulge our desires to be satisfied by food or alcohol, we are sowing to the flesh. We cannot sow these types of seeds and expect to reap a harvest of love, joy, peace, patience, kindness, goodness, faithfulness, gentleness, or self-control. We have not planted the right seeds for that kind of harvest.

How do we reap a harvest of spiritual fruit? Paul tells us to sow to the Spirit, meaning that we walk in the Spirit, obey His commands, and follow His lead. We utilize the means of grace God has given us to keep in step with the Spirit: Bible reading, prayer, fellowship with other Christians, communion, and baptism. We work out those ways of obedience—not to be saved, but because we are saved—by walking in holiness and caring for others. We do not seek salvation in our good works, though. Remember, we are justified by faith alone in Christ alone. But true saving faith will result in good works and Spirit-led living.

We sow to the Spirit when we fill our minds with what is good and true (Philippians 4:8). Walking in holiness as we follow the Spirit's lead will produce a garden full of spiritual fruit—not of our own works but of the Spirit's work of growth in us as we tend the soil faithfully with the kind of seeds that please Him. This may mean that we have to cut certain influences from our lives. If there are television shows or certain types of music that stir your affections for a sinful behavior or lustful thinking, then sowing to the Spirit requires you to remove those things from your life so that you can fill your mind with the beauty of Christ instead. Leave your sins nailed to the cross so that they continue to die—do not return to them. Instead, heed Paul's instructions to serve and care for others as you follow the Spirit's lead.

Today's passage gives two ways to do good to others. First, in verse 6, Paul exhorts us to care for our spiritual leaders. The investment of time and labor that a pastor should be giving to his study and teaching of Scripture should evoke a desire from the church to care for his needs. Both Jesus and Paul speak to the worthiness of being compensated for the work of ministry (Luke 10:7, 1 Corinthians 9:11-14, 1 Timothy 5:17-18). While both pastors and congregations must be careful to avoid any kind of abuse in the way of compensation, what Paul is encouraging here is mutual sharing. The leadership devotes time to study and prayer, sharing the teaching of Scripture with the congregation. In turn, the congregation shares their physical means with those who teach and lead them to follow Christ. Both are sowing to the Spirit when obeying the commands of Scripture.

Paul also exhorts us to do good to others, "especially for those who belong to the household of faith" (Galatians 6:10). Walking in the Spirit means caring for people from all walks of life. We are to persevere in serving our communities with the love of Christ, caring especially for other believers because they are our spiritual family through faith in Christ.

Life in the Spirit is characterized by burden-bearing, fighting for personal holiness, caring for spiritual leaders, loving our church family, and serving our communities. Because Jesus loved us and gave Himself up for us, we have the Spirit dwelling in us to empower us to walk with Him and sow the seeds that will bring about a harvest that lasts for eternity.

WE CANNOT CULTIVATE SINFUL BEHAVIOR IN OUR DAILY LIVING AND EXPECT TO SEE A HARVEST OF GOOD SPIRITUAL FRUIT.

Do you find yourself sowing to the flesh but expecting to reap a harvest of good spiritual fruit? In what ways do you need to stop sowing to the flesh. Be specific about your own thought life.

In verse 9, we are encouraged not to give up doing good. Read James 5:7-8. Why must we have patience when it comes to following Christ and sowing to the Spirit?

Do you ever feel discouraged or burned out in your service to the Lord or compassionate care for others? Write out a prayer using verse 9 as a template. Ask God to help you stay the course and continue sowing to the Spirit.

THE CROSS IS OUR ONLY HOPE

BOAST ONLY IN THE CROSS

READ GALATIANS 6:11-15

We are coming to the end of Paul's letter to the Galatians. Usually, the final words of the New Testament Epistles are laden with greetings from other believers and prayers for steadfastness. The end of Galatians, however, lacks those elements. Remember, this letter was intended to be a correction of the Judaizers' false teaching that had infiltrated the Galatian church. Paul uses his closing as one final opportunity to correct the Galatians' erroneous beliefs about circumcision and salvation. He packs quite a punch into his final plea!

Up to this point, Paul likely dictated his letter to a scribe. But in verse 11, Paul takes the pen into his own hand to assure his readers that the letter is authentic and true to his dictation. "Look at what large letters I use as I write to you in my own handwriting," he writes. While some theologians have alluded to possible physical issues with Paul's eyesight or difficulty in holding a pen (remember his maladies in 4:13-14), it is more likely that Paul meant to capture the Galatians' attention with his large letters. The modern equivalent would be to write in all capital letters or to type in bold print or underline something for emphasis. However his penmanship appeared to the Galatians as they read his letter, he wanted their utmost attention as he called them to hold fast to the true gospel message that he had leaned on throughout his entire letter. Salvation comes through faith alone in Christ alone. Circumcision, though preached by the Judaizers, cannot save anyone.

While circumcision was important in the covenant God established with Abraham in Genesis 17, the act of circumcision in and of itself is of no eternal value. The same can be said of other secondary issues we are tempted to elevate to primary importance. Baptism, for instance, is an important outward sign of an inward change, but baptism itself cannot save us. Whenever we elevate a sign over the inward change it is supposed to represent, we have erred and moved into legalism, adding to the gospel of grace. In elevating an outward sign, we bypass the heart change that must occur to be saved, and we lead people astray—just as the Judaizers were doing in Galatia. Why were the Judaizers doing this? Paul says they were ordering the Gentile believers to be circumcised and keep the law, though the Judaizers could not even keep the law themselves. Why preach circumcision then? Paul says in verses 12-13 that it was to make a good impression and avoid persecution.

If we can reduce faith to a religion of rule-following, then we do not need grace. In making Christianity a series of steps to follow, we miss salvation through faith in Christ in the attempt to avoid the persecution that comes from embracing a crucified Savior. During the time of the first-century church, persecution came primarily from the Jewish religious leaders. Preaching faith in Jesus would result in persecution much like what Stephen experienced in Acts 7 or the many kinds of suffering Paul endured for preaching the gospel. But, if you preached Christ and circumcision, you could appease the Jewish crowd and avoid suffering. This, however, was not the gospel, as Paul has labored to communicate throughout his letter. The gospel is the message of Christ crucified plus nothing. This the only message of hope and, therefore, the only message worth boasting in, according to Paul in verse 14. While taking joy in the story of Jesus's crucifixion sounds reasonable to our modern ears, it would have been jarring to Paul's readers.

Remember how shameful death by crucifixion was? In Galatians 3:13, Paul quotes Deuteronomy 21:23, saying "Cursed is everyone who is hung on a tree." We might wear cross necklaces today without much thought, but the concept of celebrating such an abominable way to die would have been unthinkable in Paul's day. The modern equivalent would be to wear a necklace or t-shirt with a guillotine or lynching mob. Imagine wearing a piece of jewelry depicting a firing squad or a gas chamber. Paul's talk of boasting in the cross would have come across just as appalling to his contemporaries. He was celebrating the most shameful way to die anyone can imagine! The crucifixion of Jesus was Paul's only hope for salvation and thus, the only thing in his life worthy of boasting about—not position, heritage, race, gender, circumcision, education, or socioeconomic status. Nothing in his life merited total devotion and glory the way Jesus's death on the cross did for Paul. And that was what Paul is calling the Galatians to consider. Faith in Jesus's saving work on the cross is our only hope for reconciliation with God, for justification, for wiping away our guilt. Nothing else in life can offer us eternal salvation.

We stake our eternity on what Jesus did on the cross. Nothing else in life gives us the hope that our crucified and risen Savior does. As a result, the allure of the world loses its shine when we place all our hope in Christ. When He is our only boast, when we are consumed with Him, when He is the one we make much of and rejoice in, then we will begin to see the effects in our feelings toward the world as we part ways with it. The temptations and desires of the flesh that we are crucifying and leaving nailed to the cross will lose their appeal over time, and we will know with certainty that what matters is that Christ has saved us and made us new. We could not do it ourselves. The cross is our only hope. We boast in what Jesus has done for us!

IF WE CAN REDUCE FAITH TO A RELIGION OF RULE-FOLLOWING, THEN WE DO NOT NEED GRACE.

As you crucify your flesh daily and boast in the death of Jesus for your salvation, you will find yourself out of step with the world. List some ways that the world has been crucified to you and you to the world (Galatians 6:14).

Read 2 Corinthians 5:16-17 and Ephesians 4:20-24. Describe what it means to be a new creation in Christ.

In your own words, explain what it means to boast in the cross of Jesus Christ.

WE CANNOT EARN GRACE,
WE CAN ONLY RECEIVE IT

THE MARKS OF JESUS

READ GALATIANS 6:16-18

From the greeting to the benediction, Paul's letter to the church in Galatia is saturated with grace. Were we to reduce the message of Galatians to one idea or theme, it would be grace, all grace. Salvation is a gift of God's unmerited favor. We cannot save ourselves by accomplishing good works or keeping certain rituals. We cannot earn grace; we can only receive it. The gospel is good news for us because God has made a way for us to be forgiven, reconciled, and made new. He has done this through Jesus, and we are recipients of His transformative grace when we believe in Jesus's sacrifice for our sins on the cross.

Paul closes his letter with a traditional Jewish benediction of peace and mercy, but he evokes this benediction for "all those who follow this standard," calling them "the Israel of God." What is the standard, and who is the Israel of God? Looking back at verses 14-15, we see Paul's summary of the gospel: boasting in the cross of Christ and being a new creation. Going back even further in Galatians, we learned that those who belong to Christ are Abraham's offspring (3:7-9, 14, 16, 29; 4:28). Paul also told us in Romans 5:1 that "since we have been declared righteous by faith, we have peace with God through our Lord Jesus Christ." We can conclude that Paul's invocation of peace and mercy is for all who have believed in Jesus for salvation and who hold to the true message of the gospel of grace. The people of God are those who have been justified by faith in Jesus and have become heirs of the promises to Abraham. Those people make up the body of Christ—the church— and must hold to the gospel and boast only in Jesus's death on the cross. Scripture is our standard for life and truth. If we have believed in Jesus for the forgiveness of our sins, we are part of "the Israel of God." We are members of God's family and recipients of His promises.

We enjoy peace with God and one another when we hold to the standard of biblical truth. We must know the Word, live by it, saturate our minds with it, and be transformed by it. Christianity cannot be reduced to adhering to a code of ethics or keeping religious rituals. It is not about external behavior or rule-following. True Christianity is a transformation of the heart that happens when we believe in Jesus, take up our cross, and follow Him. Following Christ means rejecting a life of sinful desires and walking in the Spirit instead. Following Christ means emulating Him, sharing in His sufferings and His glory. This is what Paul refers to when he talks about bearing on his body "the marks of Jesus" in verse 17.

The Greek word for marks in verse 17 is *stigmata*, which refers to the branding of a slave. Paul's physical sufferings for the gospel branded him as a slave of Christ. In 2 Corinthians 11:23-28, Paul gives a long list of the sufferings he has endured for the gospel: severe beatings, stonings, shipwreck; dangers from rivers, robbers, Jews, Gentiles, and false teachers; dangers at sea, in the wilderness, and in cities; hardship, sleeplessness, hunger, thirst, cold, as well as the daily pressures of ministry. At least some of his sufferings were experienced before he wrote this letter to the Galatians (Acts 14:19). These things Paul endured joyfully, even when beaten and jailed for preaching the gospel. The accusations by the Judaizers or any other false teachers could not hold up. Paul's very body was branded with his suffering for the true gospel of Jesus. In a sense, Paul is drawing attention to the markings of a slave of Christ. Circumcision does not brand us as slaves of Christ; suffering does. That is not to say we should go out looking for suffering. But we must be prepared for it, ready to stand firm on the gospel of grace when the pressures of false teachings tempt us to sway in another, easier direction. We are guaranteed to suffer as Christians because we follow a Savior who suffered. Paul said that "all who want to live a godly life in Christ Jesus will be persecuted" (2 Timothy 3:12). When persecution comes, will we be prepared to stand firm?

We might not experience the kinds of physical sufferings in our context today that Paul experienced, but we will face persecutions if we cling to the cross of Christ. It is not popular to believe that man is sinful, that certain lifestyles or habits are at odds with Christ-following, or that the only way to heaven is through faith in Jesus. Will we gladly bear the marks of suffering in our lives when our neighbor or co-worker or friend disagrees with biblical truth? Will we sacrifice our reputation or time or money to share the gospel in a world that is hostile to its message? The Apostle Peter said that we should not be surprised by suffering as Christians but rather, that we should "rejoice as you share in the sufferings of Christ, so that you may also rejoice with great joy when His glory is revealed" (1 Peter 4:13). The secret to joyfully and patiently enduring suffering for the sake of Christ is to keep our eyes on what is coming. Those who share in the sufferings of Christ, who bear His marks on their body, also share in the grace and glory of Christ in their spirits. Our suffering may be hard, but it is temporary and will be eclipsed by "an absolutely incomparable eternal weight of glory (2 Corinthians 4:17). We can gladly bear the marks of Christ knowing that we will also share in His glory forever.

TRUE CHRISTIANITY IS A TRANSFORMATION OF THE HEART THAT HAPPENS WHEN WE BELIEVE IN JESUS, TAKE UP OUR CROSS, AND FOLLOW HIM.

Why is it so important to read, study, and live by the words of God in Scripture?
How does this help us to know peace and mercy?

Read John 16:33, Romans 5:3-5, 2 Timothy 3:12, James 1:2, and 1 Peter 4:12-13.
What do we learn about suffering and trial as Christians?

How does your life bear the marks of Jesus? If you have not experienced physical persecution,
think about the marks of Jesus on your friendships, reputation, bank account, and time.

LIVE BY FAITH

GRACE AND FAITH

READ GALATIANS 1-6

The book of Galatians is about grace and faith from start to finish. From the day we first believe the gospel of Jesus until the day we see Him face to face, we live by grace through faith in the One who gave Himself for us on the cross. There is no part of our salvation or sanctification that is accomplished by our own strength or with our works. Galatians reminds us of this truth from beginning to end.

Paul wrote to the Galatian Christians to both correct erroneous theology and to exhort them to keep the true gospel at the forefront of their minds. We would do well in our contemporary context to keep both Paul's correction and exhortation in mind as we follow the same Savior the Galatians followed. God has preserved the good news of salvation through faith in Jesus for us. The Galatians could not earn their salvation, and neither can we. We must all, from every imaginable background, come to salvation the same way—not by works but by grace through faith in Jesus. The gospel has always been a message of grace and faith, and it always will be.

Paul's correction of false teaching within the Galatian church provides a needed warning for us today. There will always be people who pervert the Scriptures, twisting the truth of the gospel into something that downplays grace and demands prideful performances instead. We must remain vigilant against any form of legalism that slips into the church. The heart of man is prideful at its core and will always look for ways to earn or perform in order to be saved (Jeremiah 17:9). We must watch out for the subtle ways that we turn the grace of God into something we must earn. Any teaching that requires something other than faith in Christ for salvation is a false gospel, and as Paul taught in Galatians 1:6-7, those false gospels are no gospel at all. Salvation through works is not good news for us; we could never be good enough to justify ourselves. That is why Jesus's perfect sacrifice on the cross in our place is such good news. It is a gift of grace.

How do we guard against the infiltration of false gospels? We hold fast to the true gospel. This means we must know the message of Jesus crucified on the cross in our place for our sins. We must make a study of the teachings of the prophets and apostles who were appointed by God and inspired by the Holy Spirit. To recognize false teaching and stand firmly against it, we must be very familiar with what Scripture does teach. Daily Bible reading might feel like a chore at times, but the regular intake of Scripture renews our minds and develops discernment in our hearts. When we are familiar with the truth, we will be able to recognize false teaching and stand against it. Regular examination of God's Word is how we stand firm.

While we may never be tempted to add the practice of circumcision to the requirements for salvation like the Galatians did, we may be tempted to add other requirements to the gospel. Or, we may turn grace into an excuse to freely indulge our sinful desires. Paul's letter is still relevant and applicable today. As we hold to the gift of God's grace, we must, like the Galatians, be careful not to use grace as a license to sin. Living by faith means being led by the Spirit, putting to death our fleshly desires, and seeking to obey the commands of Christ instead. We have been made new, and as new creatures in Christ, we leave our former ways of living at the cross (Galatians 5:24). The Holy Spirit lives in our hearts, and as children of God, we are empowered to obey and run after what pleases God rather than what pleases man. The Spirit enables us to love one another, to carry each other's burdens, to restore those who are wandering away in sin, and to do good to everyone, especially to our family of faith.

Living by faith as the children of God gives us true freedom from sin. God's grace does not leave us as we are but makes us more and more like Christ as we walk with the Spirit each day. We no longer have to live like slaves to sin but can live as free children of God. This is what Jesus accomplished for us at the cross that we could never do for ourselves. He has paid the debt we owed and given us His righteousness instead. What do we do with such a gift of grace? We walk forward in faith, proclaiming this gift of grace to the world around us while we wait for the return of our Savior who loves us and gave Himself for us. The gospel of grace enables us to live by faith until we see Jesus face to face.

GOD'S GRACE DOES NOT LEAVE US AS WE ARE BUT MAKES US MORE AND MORE LIKE CHRIST AS WE WALK WITH THE SPIRIT EACH DAY.

What truth(s) from Galatians have encouraged you the most?

What truth(s) from Galatians have convicted you the most?

Summarize the core message of Galatians in your own words.
What major themes stood out to you?

BUT AS FOR ME, I WILL
NEVER BOAST ABOUT
ANYTHING EXCEPT THE
CROSS OF OUR LORD JESUS
CHRIST. THE WORLD HAS
BEEN CRUCIFIED TO ME
THROUGH THE CROSS,
AND I TO THE WORLD.

—

GALATIANS 6:14

Paraphrase the passage from this week.

What did you observe from this week's text about God and His character?

What does this week's passage reveal about the condition of mankind and yourself?

How does this passage point to the gospel?

How should you respond to this passage? What specific action steps can you take this week to apply this passage?

Write a prayer in response to your study of God's Word. Adore God for who He is, confess sins that He has revealed in your own life, ask Him to empower you to walk in obedience, and pray for anyone who came to mind as you studied.

WHAT IS THE GOSPEL?

THANK YOU FOR READING AND ENJOYING THIS STUDY WITH US! WE ARE
ABUNDANTLY GRATEFUL FOR THE WORD OF GOD, THE INSTRUCTION WE
GLEAN FROM IT, AND THE EVER-GROWING UNDERSTANDING ABOUT
GOD'S CHARACTER FROM IT. WE ARE ALSO THANKFUL THAT SCRIPTURE
CONTINUALLY POINTS TO ONE THING IN INNUMERABLE WAYS: THE GOSPEL.

We remember our brokenness when we read about the fall of Adam and Eve in the garden of Eden (Genesis 3), when sin entered into a perfect world and maimed it. We remember the necessity that something innocent must die to pay for our sin when we read about the atoning sacrifices in the Old Testament. We read that we have all sinned and fallen short of the glory of God (Romans 3:23) and that the penalty for our brokenness, the wages of our sin, is death (Romans 6:23). We all are in need of grace and mercy, but most importantly, we all need a Savior.

We consider the goodness of God when we realize that He did not plan to leave us in this dire state. We see His promise to buy us back from the clutches of sin and death in Genesis 3:15. And we see that promise accomplished with Jesus Christ on the cross. Jesus Christ knew no sin yet became sin so that we might become righteous through His sacrifice (2 Corinthians 5:21). Jesus was tempted in every way that we are and lived sinlessly. He was reviled yet still yielded Himself for our sake, that we may have life abundant in Him. Jesus lived the perfect life that we could not live and died the death that we deserved.

The gospel is profound yet simple. There are many mysteries in it that we can never exhaust this side of heaven, but there is still overwhelming weight to its implications in this life. The gospel is the telling of our sinfulness and God's goodness, and this gracious gift compels a response. We are saved by grace through faith, which means

that we rest with faith in the grace that Jesus Christ displayed on the cross (Ephesians 2:8-9). We cannot save ourselves from our brokenness or do any amount of good works to merit God's favor, but we can have faith that what Jesus accomplished in His death, burial, and resurrection was more than enough for our salvation and our eternal delight. When we accept God, we are commanded to die to our self and our sinful desires and live a life worthy of the calling we have received (Ephesians 4:1). The gospel compels us to be sanctified, and in so doing, we are conformed to the likeness of Christ Himself. This is hope. This is redemption. This is the gospel.

SCRIPTURE TO REFERENCE:

GENESIS 3:15   *I will put hostility between you and the woman, and between your offspring and her offspring. He will strike your head, and you will strike his heel.*

ROMANS 3:23   *For all have sinned and fall short of the glory of God.*

ROMANS 6:23   *For the wages of sin is death, but the gift of God is eternal life in Christ Jesus our Lord.*

2 CORINTHIANS 5:21   *He made the one who did not know sin to be sin for us, so that in him we might become the righteousness of God.*

EPHESIANS 2:8-9   *For you are saved by grace through faith, and this is not from yourselves; it is God's gift — not from works, so that no one can boast.*

EPHESIANS 4:1   *Therefore I, the prisoner in the Lord, urge you to walk worthy of the calling you have received,*

*Thank you for studying
God's Word with us!*

CONNECT WITH US

@thedailygraceco

@kristinschmucker

CONTACT US

info@thedailygraceco.com

SHARE

#thedailygraceco

#lampandlight

VISIT US ONLINE

www.thedailygraceco.com

MORE DAILY GRACE

The Daily Grace App
Daily Grace Podcast